COMPLETE SURRENDER

COMPLETE SURRENDER

A Biography of Eric Liddell Olympic Gold Medallist and Missionary

Julian Wilson

Authentic

Copyright © 1996, 2012 Julian Wilson

18 17 16 15 14 13 12   7 6 5 4 3 2 1

First published 1996 by Monarch Publications
This revised edition published 2012 by Authentic Media Limited
52 Presley Way, Crownhill, Milton Keynes, MK8 0ES
www.authenticmedia.co.uk

The right of Julian Wilson to be identified as the Author of this
Work has been asserted by him in accordance with the Copyright,
Designs and Patents Act 1988.

British Library Cataloguing-in-Publication Data

A catalogue record for this book is available from the
British Library

ISBN 978-1-86024-841-2

Scripture quotations are taken from the
HOLY BIBLE, KING JAMES VERSION

Cover design by Paul Airy (www.designleft.co.uk)
Printed and bound by CPI Cox and Wyman, Reading, RG1 8EX

To Lian

CONTENTS

ACKNOWLEDGEMENTS

I am most grateful to all those who have contributed anecdotes, memories, letters, articles, photographs and other material that has enhanced this biography so richly. In particular, I would like to thank Professor Neil Campbell, Bill Cranfield, Dr George Graham-Cummings, Dr Peggy Judge, Reverend John Keddie, Sir Arthur Marshall, Dr Kenneth McAll, David Michell, Jenny Somerville, Kari Torjesen Malcolm and Charles Walker.

Many thanks to Lord David Puttnam for providing an excellent foreword.

I also owe a debt of gratitude to Reverend D.P. Thompson, who wrote *Scotland's Greatest Athlete* (The Research Unit, 1971). His book has been invaluable in the writing of this one.

FOREWORD

My first encounter with the story of Eric Liddell came
about entirely by accident. Cooped up in a rented house
in Los Angeles and casting about for something to read,
I chanced upon *The Official History of the Olympic Games*
(published by Franklin Mint, 1976), gathering dust on a
bookshelf. I love reading record books and quickly
found myself entranced by it, and most particularly by
the events surrounding the 1924 Olympics. It seemed to
me that it would all make a terrific basis for a film.

For some time, I'd been looking for material which
had a moral and allegorical resonance capable of trans-
porting an audience far beyond the tarnished aspirations
of our own altogether more petulant age. Liddell's story
was perfect. His idealism, his passion to communicate,
his evangelical drive – such values it seemed to me had
been almost obliterated by the insidious spread of contemporary cynicism. Yet they were the values I'd been
brought up on and to which I felt instinctively drawn. I
suppose in many ways Liddell was the kind of person
who, in my heart of hearts, I'd always dreamed of being.

What's more, in tackling the story of Eric Liddell and
his 'counterpoint' Harold Abrahams, we had to address

a whole range of issues – class, race and religion – which have haunted me all my adult life. At root, *Chariots of Fire* is a film about a man who lived by the rule of honour in preference to that of convenience. Eric Liddell's instinct was always to do what's right. That's the quality that shines most powerfully through both his sporting career and, of course, his later work as a missionary.

In our own age, by contrast, the prevailing instinct is inevitably to do what's most convenient or, to be more precise, what's expedient. In his preface to *The Disciplines of the Christian Life* (SPCK Classics, 2009), Liddell wrote of wanting 'to help people apply their [Christian] knowledge to daily life; to live according to the light they have'.

Looking at many contemporary heroes, it's clear that their light has long since been extinguished; in some cases it's as if it never existed at all. In the 'culture of celebrity' which now pervades all aspects of our lives, it's enough to be measured by fame and money alone. Think of sport – or, indeed, of cinema. Both are forms of human expression which have immense power to influence the way we lead our lives, not least because they create attractive heroes and heroines with whom people all over the world can instantly identify. Yet many contemporary icons of sport and cinema are fairly tawdry figures, whose arrogant and demeaning behaviour speaks of nothing more exalted than the desire to enrich themselves irrespective of the cost to their dignity.

Eric Liddell, by contrast, recognised that those who live amid the glare of publicity have hard choices to make about the way they lead their lives, choices which entail considerable personal responsibility. It's my belief that film-makers and all those who work with them are faced with the same kind of choices and responsibilities – indeed it's incumbent on them to realise that the films they choose to make have an effect on the workaday lives of the audience and their ability to deal with the world they inhabit. Liddell himself spoke of 'the art of living a Christian life' knowing it was something to be worked at, something to be striven for in the face of temptations which offer an altogether more convenient way of conducting one's affairs.

As this admirable biography demonstrates, few lives have more to teach us about the virtues of honour and probity as the guiding principles for a practical code of ethics. That's why, long after the names of most of the current band of sporting heroes have sunk into obscurity, it's my belief that the memory of Eric Liddell is likely to endure. It will endure as a monument to the integrity of a man who, no matter what temptations might have been strewn in his path, always steered his life by that special interior light with which he was blessed. In helping to keep the memory of that light alive, Julian Wilson has performed a truly valuable service to us all.

Lord David Puttnam

CHINA:
PLACES OF SIGNIFICANCE IN ERIC LIDDELL'S LIFE

INTRODUCTION

'Eric Liddell, missionary, died in occupied China at the end of World War II. All of Scotland mourned.'

So reads the brief epitaph at the end of the film *Chariots of Fire* (dir. Hugh Hudson, 1981). Like me, you may have been intrigued as to how Eric Liddell came to be in China, what he did there and how he died. This you will discover as you read on.

What explains the legacy of Eric Liddell? Why should the memory of a man who won but a single Olympic gold medal more than 90 years ago be so enduring? His achievements were noble but not exceptional. Yes, he refused to run on a Sunday, but Christians throughout the centuries have made far greater sacrifices; many have given up their lives for their faith.

Shy, diffident and initially a mediocre speaker, Liddell was, except for his performances on the track, a man of average ability who did extraordinary deeds through he who dwelled within him. 'He was not particularly clever and not conspicuously able, but he was good. He wasn't a great leader or an inspired thinker, but he knew what he ought to do and did it,' wrote one who observed him. Yet it was his very 'ordinariness' that made him so magnetic.

As the late Ian Charleson, who played Liddell in the film *Chariots of Fire*, remarked, 'He just talked about real things – about himself and his faith and what he did that morning.'

With an honesty and sincerity that shone through his faltering oratory, allied to a simple gospel message, he profoundly touched the hearts of many, whether it were the young men who heard him speak during the Christian student crusades of the 1920s, peasants on the North China Plain or those who had lost all hope in the Japanese internment camp where he died of a brain tumour in February 1945.

His love for humanity, regardless of colour, class or creed, was ever enduring. It was, according to one of Liddell's flatmates, like God's love. He had a passion for perfection both in his personal life and on the running track, but could accept imperfection in others, refusing to pass judgement and always searching for the spark of good in all.

Yet he was not religious or, as his wife Florence put it, 'holy, holy'. He loved the good life, was a notorious practical joker and was once observed doing the Charleston with great gusto in Paris before the 1924 Olympics. And there was always that quiet smile, those twinkling blue eyes and gentle sense of humour; a humour, according to Florence, that was so deadpan that you had to watch his eyes closely to determine whether he was joking or not.

What was his secret? The complete surrender of his life to God. 'Absolute surrender' was a phrase he often uttered. 'He was literally,' observed a colleague, 'God-controlled, in his thoughts, judgements, actions, words, to an extent I have never seen surpassed, and rarely seen equalled. Every morning he rose early to pray and read the Bible in silence: talking and listening to God, pondering the day ahead and often smiling as if at a private joke.'

Thus to the question: Why the continued interest in Eric Liddell? Is it because he represents a nostalgic perception of a gentler, more noble, more innocent age of honour and chivalry, self-sacrifice and moral rectitude, even if such an age never really existed? Or is it simply because he embodied what most of us, if we are honest, yearn to be but never seem quite able to attain?

In the twenty-first century, the world cries out for men and women of the calibre of Eric Liddell: people of love, honour, courage and selflessness; who will practise what they preach; who are willing to take a stand for truth and righteousness; who will mount up with wings as eagles.

1

FIRST AMONG EQUALS

On a stiflingly hot Parisian afternoon in July 1924, six athletes lined up for the start of the Olympic 400 metres. In the outside lane was Scottish sprint sensation Eric Liddell. The year before, Liddell had set the athletics world alight when he came within one hundredth of a second of the 100 yards world record, establishing himself as one of the favourites to snatch the gold medal in the blue ribbon event of the Games, the 100 metres. A cruel twist of fate was to deny him the opportunity to compete for that coveted prize. The heats of the 100 metres were on a Sunday and Liddell, a devout Christian who considered the Sabbath as sacred, refused to run. For this act of principle, he suffered the vilification of the British athletics establishment, the press and the public. There were cries of, 'He's a traitor to his country!' These accusations wounded Liddell deeply although, characteristically, he never let it show.

Undaunted, he turned instead to the 400 metres, a distance at which he was a still a novice, but in which he had proved his mettle at a meeting held in July 1923 between England, Scotland and Ireland. Bundled off the track almost immediately after the start, Liddell came storming back to win after losing eighteen metres in what was described by *The Scotsman* as 'one of the greatest races ever run'.

Although given little chance of success, he had fought his way to the Olympic final, improving steadily with each round. Now, as he carefully placed his feet in the starting holes he had dug in the cinder track, and crouched crab-like in the starting position staring determinedly ahead down the first straight, he had the chance to prove his critics wrong. Never before had a natural sprinter won the Olympic 400 metres, and alongside Liddell were three men who had already broken the world record in the heats.

As the wail of the Scottish Cameron Highlanders' bagpipes, who had struck up the rousing 'Scotland the Brave' to inspire Liddell, faded away, a deathly hush descended on the Colombes Stadium.

'To your marks!' cried the Olympic official.

In the outside lane, Eric Liddell jerked instinctively half-upright. The pause seemed to last for an eternity as every muscle in his body tensed, sweat dripping from his forehead and trickling uncomfortably down his spine in the intense heat.

Then suddenly, shattering the eerie silence, the starting pistol cracked. Like a catapult drawn back to breaking point and then released, Liddell shot out of his starting holes as though he were running the 100 metres sprint. He flashed past the 200 metre mark in 22.2 seconds – only 0.6 of a second slower than the winner of the 200 metres two days before.

'Surely he can't keep this pace up,' whispered people in the stands in awe. 'He's bound to tie up in the home straight.'

As Liddell entered the final turn and into the home straight, he was only two metres ahead of the American,

Horatio Fitch. For a few anxious seconds, it looked as though he was beginning to falter. Then, somehow, he tapped hidden reserves of strength and stamina. Knees pumping, arms flailing, his mouth open, head thrust far back, Liddell surged further ahead of Fitch and burst through the tape five metres ahead. His winning time of 47.6 seconds was a new world and Olympic record. The announcement over the tannoy was almost drowned out by rapturous applause as the ecstatic British contingent in the crowd celebrated his historic victory. Against all the odds, he had triumphed!

The new Olympic 400-metres champion, who now stood shaking hands and posing self-consciously hands on hips for the film cameras, was relatively short at 1.75 metres (5 feet 9 inches). Deep-chested and muscular, his gait was springy if not bandy-legged. In looks he took after his father, James Dunlop Liddell, his chin firm and dimpled, his long face made longer by fair hair which, even at the age of 22, was rapidly receding, a condition his disappointed mother attributed to too many hot showers. What distinguished an otherwise ordinary-looking face were his eyes, intense steel-blue and twinkling, and a delightful, winsome smile.

James Liddell came from the village of Drymen near Loch Lomond, bordering the Highlands of Scotland. His father was greatly esteemed in the village, where he kept a grocer's shop. As a sideline he operated a small wagonette, known locally as 'Liddell's machine', to and from the railway station, about a mile away, to pick up passengers. Bearded and laconic, he always wore a high bowler hat as he perched atop his cart, his white pony ambling along at walking pace.

The Liddells were a highly respected family, renowned for their evangelistic fervour at a time and in a place when charismatic evangelism was uncommon.

'I have a vague recollection of a group of evangelists who used to hold meetings in the village square. I think they belonged to the Faith Mission,' recalled a resident of Drymen. 'The Liddells braved the criticism of their neighbours by coming out boldly in support of these visitors, singing Moody and Sankey hymns, etc.'

James Liddell began his working life as a draper's apprentice, but he was clearly destined for a higher calling.

'From the first day we met he has stood as my ideal of Christian brotherliness,' remarked a close friend. 'He had such a big heart. There was no shadow of meanness or narrowness in him. He was never so happy as when doing something for others.' After meeting a minister of the Scottish Congregational Church while on holiday, Liddell was inspired to pursue a more spiritual vocation: to become a missionary on the foreign field.

In 1893 he met Mary Reddin at a Sunday school picnic in Stirling. Quiet and gentle, with her dark hair swept up into a bun, she worked as a nurse in Glasgow and was convalescing with friends in Stirling after an illness. They were both 22 when they met and got engaged soon afterwards. They were not to marry, however, for another six years, while Liddell studied theology at the Congregational College in Glasgow in order to be ordained, and Mary continued nursing.

In 1898, he applied to the London Missionary Society (LMS) and was offered a position at their mission in Mongolia, northern China, as a probationary missionary. Liddell wanted to marry before sailing for China, but the LMS shrewdly required him to prove himself and pass his exams in Chinese before agreeing to the expense of sending his fiancée out to join him.

The Reverend James Liddell duly lived up to their expectations, passing his Chinese exams in record time and establishing a reputation as a compassionate and peace-loving man admired and respected by both Chinese and Westerner alike. With his post confirmed, James sent for Mary Reddin and they were married in Shanghai Cathedral on 22 October 1899.

It was not an auspicious time either to get married or to be a foreign missionary in China. Latent xenophobia fuelled by years of humiliation and exploitation at the hands of the European powers erupted in June 1900 with the infamous Boxer Rising. Named after the 'League of Righteous and Harmonious Fists', the Boxers exhorted the peasantry to rise up and expel all foreigners, particularly Christian missionaries. The Boxer edict stated: 'The Catholic and Protestant religions being insolent to the gods, and extinguishing sanctity, rendering no obedience to Buddha, and enraging Heaven and Earth, the rain clouds no longer visit us; but eight million Spirit Soldiers will descend from Heaven to sweep the Empire clean of all foreigners.'

In the carnage that followed the assassination of the German ambassador in Beijing, more than 200 Western missionaries and approximately 30,000 Chinese Christians were slaughtered.

'In the surrounding streets,' wrote an observer, 'hundreds, perhaps thousands of Christians were butchered.' Next day (15 June), patrols of American, Russian, British and German marines went out and brought in survivors, shooting any Boxers they met. Dr G.E. Morrison, *The Times* correspondent in Beijing who went with them, witnessed 'awful sights . . . women and children hacked to pieces, men trussed like fowls, with noses and ears cut off and eyes gouged out'.

One American missionary in China wrote home in great distress. 'How am I to write all the horrible details of these days? The dear ones of Chouyang, seven in all, including our lovely girls, were taken prisoner and brought to Taiyuan in irons, and there by the Governor's orders, beheaded, together with the Taiyuan friends, thirty-three souls. The following days the Roman Catholic priests and nuns of Taiyuan were also beheaded, ten souls yesterday. Three weeks after these had perished, our mission at Taku was attacked, and our six friends there, and several brave Christians who stood by them, were beheaded. We are now waiting for a call home . . .'

With the unrest spreading like wildfire throughout northern China and with Mary pregnant, the Liddells, in fear of their lives, were forced to flee Mongolia for the comparative safety of the LMS compound in Shanghai, where Mary gave birth to their eldest son, Robert Victor. Three months later, James returned to Mongolia, leaving Mary at the LMS compound in Tianjin (then known as Tientsin), to try and discover what had become of the Chinese Christians he had left behind.

'For four months,' writes Mary, 'he was touring Mongolia, with Colonel Wei and 200 soldiers, and I could get no word from him. I wish he had written down his experiences. He had a tale to tell that was thrilling, but he never attempted to keep a diary. Life was too strenuous and it seemed we must just live a day at a time, as we never knew what would happen next. All winter was a difficult time, murders and horrible things happening.'

Sixteen months later, on 16 January 1902, Eric was born. The intention was to christen him 'Henry Eric Liddell', but on the way to church for his baptism it was pointed out that the initials spelt 'H.E.L.' – hardly appropriate for the son of a missionary – and his name was quickly changed to 'Eric Henry Liddell'.

With the mission in Mongolia no longer tenable, James Liddell was posted to Xiaochang (formerly

Siaochang), one of two missions operated by the LMS on the Great Plain of North China, home to a teeming population of about ten million living in myriad villages which were described by one observer as being 'as close to one another as currants in a rich cake'. The climate was dry, with temperatures ranging from 43 °C (110 °F) to below zero in winter. Missionary activity had been in progress for decades and the nucleus of a Chinese Church had been established.

Mary joined her husband when Eric was old enough to travel, and it was here, in 1903, that Jenny, the Liddells' third child was born (a fourth, Ernest, was born in 1912). Before she died in 1994, Jenny still had vivid memories of family life during those early days at the mission:

'The LMS station in Xiaochang consisted then of four large houses in a row. They had verandahs on two sides, both upstairs and down. Behind the houses were the church, a boys' school and a girls' school. These were surrounded by a high wall built of mud, with a large gate closed at night.'

She recalled a devoted Chinese amah, who, unable to pronounce Eric's name correctly, called him 'Yellee'. Eric and his brother Rob, in their quilted jackets, would romp with their pet goats and kittens, speaking fluent Chinese with their playmates and basking in the undivided attention of a family far from home.

Once, Jenny remembers, Eric was very ill. 'He was fed on nothing but Valentine's Meat Juice for a time. Mother never left his side, and it was only her devoted nursing that pulled him through. For a time afterwards, he was very stiff on his legs, and one lady was heard to remark, "That boy will never be able to run again." How little did she know what lay ahead!'

When the summer heat was at its most intense, Mary Liddell and the family would escape for two or three months to the cool of the seaside resort of Beidaihe (formerly Pei-Tai-Ho), Shandong Province, where the mission owned a few cottages. In later years, it became the place where Eric Liddell took his own family for holidays.

In 1907, after nine tempestuous years in China, James Liddell received his first furlough and the family returned to Drymen in Scotland. It was the last time that Eric, who was five, would see Xiaochang until he became a missionary there himself in 1937.

It was this short period of family life, despite being interrupted by the strife and turbulence in China, that was the first great formative influence on the shaping of Eric Liddell's character. As a family friend was to comment after Liddell's death, 'No one who knew Liddell's father and mother, no one who had been a guest in their home, who had sensed its atmosphere and its outlook, and had become aware of the spirit which permeated it, could be in any doubt that it was from his parents he got his inspiration and ideals.'

The Liddells rented a furnished house in Drymen, James Liddell's home village, and stayed there before returning to China in 1908. But before they left, it was necessary to make arrangements for Rob and Eric's schooling, which had already begun at the village school. The natural choice, considering the boys' background, was the School for the Sons of Missionaries, located in Blackheath, London, before it moved to another area of London, Mottingham, in 1912, and was renamed Eltham College.

Their mother's last glimpse of Rob and Eric before she sailed for China was of two little boys in the school playground, far below the level of the road on which she stood, so completely absorbed in a game of cricket that they were oblivious of their mother leaving. That night, little Eric, not yet seven, wept himself to sleep.

Initially, Liddell made little impression at the school. 'When he first joined us,' recalled one of his old masters, 'Eric was very shy, and physically rather "weedy". He missed his parents greatly, and sheltered as far as possible under his brother's protection. But a kindness would always bring from him a grateful glance, and gradually his innate courtesy overcame his bashfulness.' So bashful was he it seems that when the local girls' school challenged Eltham College to a tennis match, Liddell dropped out because he was too shy to visit the school. Quiet and unobtrusive, he was the natural choice to play the Dormouse in *Alice in Wonderland*. His acting debut brought the house down, and from then on he was dubbed 'The Mouse'.

As well as his thespian and sporting activities, Eric was involved in the religious life of the school. True to form, he was too diffident to take part in discussions during the Bible classes he attended regularly. 'But,' remarked the master who took the classes, 'I always knew that however poor the fare I brought to it might be, I could count on an encouraging half-smile, half-nod, when I looked his way.'

Painfully shy he may have remained, but physically he was developing rapidly, responding to an outdoor regime introduced by the Headmaster, W.B. Hayward. Within a couple of years, fresh air and two terms of rugby, with often three or four games a week, had made a new man of Liddell.

Hayward, a strong disciplinarian, and his successor, George Robertson, shared a belief in the benefits of Christianity combined with sport for building character, courage, manliness and team spirit. Their doctrine was epitomised by another great Victorian headmaster, H.H. Almond, who declared passionately, 'Why, oh why, cannot there be a holy alliance between the athlete and the Christian; an alliance against the common enemies of both, against intemperance and indolence, and dissipation, and effeminacy, and aesthetic voluptuousness, and heartless cynicism, and all the unnatural and demoralising elements in our social life?'

Inculcating Christian and sporting values was a task made easier for the masters by virtue of the pupils' backgrounds. Nearly all the boys had missionaries as parents and were well-versed in Christian principles. Disparities between pupils were few; most came from families with little money. 'We reckoned in pennies,' wrote one pupil, 'and often had none of them for long periods. Many of us remained at school through the holidays; by modern standards we seldom went out. And so we came to know each other intimately, like brothers, and we formed each other. The school was our family, and did for us not only a school's job, but much of what a family circle does for those who have one.' For Rob and Eric, Christmas holidays were often spent with friends of the LMS; Easter at the school; and only the long summer vacations were deemed worthy of the expense of sending the boys to faraway Drymen or to stay with relatives in Berwick-upon-Tweed on the English–Scottish border.

This environment, in which Eric Liddell grew up and matured, was one which, despite its family ambience, betrayed many of the trappings of a typical English public school of the time, with hallowed traditions and wholesome if interminably dull cuisine: for breakfast, porridge and bread and butter or dripping with occasional jam or marmalade; for supper, a huge doorstep of bread and butter or dripping. Young Eric fell foul of the kitchen on at least one occasion when he pertinently demonstrated what he thought of the food. Asking to be excused from supper one evening, he deposited the indigestible mass still in his mouth into a waste paper bin. Punishment was swiftly administered.

Popular among his peers and schoolmasters alike, Liddell may have been quiet and shy but he was never aloof. 'My own memory of him,' wrote a fellow schoolboy, 'is of a lion-hearted but always modest companion, always popular, but from early days independent, self-reliant and a little detached. I never remember him having a bosom pal.'

'Before he had been six months with us,' recalled a master, 'I was struck by his absolute straightforwardness. No matter what hot water he got into, he would, when questioned, tell a perfectly straight tale – always, however, one that did not incriminate any comrades in the distress he might have.'

Even George Robertson was impressed by Eric's innate qualities. 'Entirely without vanity, he was enormously popular. Very early he showed signs of real character. His standing had been set for him long before he came to the school. There was no pride or fuss about him, but he knew what he stood for.'

This is not to say that Liddell was beyond reproach. He indulged in his share of schoolboy pranks, such as the occasion when he observed the headmaster 'breaking' his own rule forbidding boys from cycling in the school quadrangle and shouted from a classroom window: 'Hey, no cycling there!' His voice was recognised and he was sent to bed without supper.

There was even a sneaking suspicion that Liddell was involved in the ragging (making fun) of younger boys, despite his cherubic innocence. One day in class, the headmaster caught a glimpse of a defiant look in his eyes that he had not noticed before.

'Liddell,' he said, 'I am beginning to think you are not as good as you look.'

It's possible that Liddell was involved or at least an interested bystander in a ragging which perhaps only the sons of missionaries could have conceived: a terrified new boy was lowered slowly from an upper window, while above, the Order of the Burial of the Dead at Sea was read with great reverence. To his credit, at only eight years old and at the request of another pupil, he stepped in and prevented the ragging of a newcomer who was being forced to run a gauntlet of blows from knotted handkerchiefs, challenging an established ritual in the presence of boys of ten and eleven.

Never one to suffer snobbery and injustice for long, a fellow pupil recalls his humorous resistance to bullying, supercilious masters, often answering questions with a strong tinge of satire followed by a disarming smile. This side of his character – a love of playing practical jokes and a sense of humour that deflated any attempt at pomposity – took the heat out of many a confrontational situation, whether it involved his schoolmasters or battle-hardened Japanese soldiers in occupied northern China.

Not an outstanding scholar – he once complained to his sister Jenny that he did not think much of the lessons – Eric's talent lay on the sports field. Whether it was rugby, running, cricket or a host of other sports, Liddell excelled, as witnessed by his rapid rise to prominence at Eltham from 'weedy' new boy to one of the school's sporting stars. In the space of two years, he became captain of both the rugby First XV and cricket First XI, holder of the school's 100 yards (91.44 metres) at seventeen with a time of 10.2 seconds and winner of the Blackheath Cup in 1918 for the best all-round sportsman of the year.

Liddell's achievements, however, must be viewed in the light of the school's size (less than 200 pupils in 1916) and the exigencies of the First World War, which drew many senior boys away from Eltham to the trenches of Flanders, making it easier for him to shine. Such was the shortage of older boys that Liddell was appointed captain of the rugby team at only sixteen. Nevertheless, his progress between 1916 and 1918 was prodigious. In cricket, not his best game, the 1916 edition of the Eltham College magazine, *The Elthamian*, records that Liddell, 'Does not put enough force into his strokes; is too fond of tipping balls. A slow, but good length bowler, seldom needed. A good field and throws in well from point. Should do well next year.'

By 1918, the magazine is more enthusiastic, 'A good all-round cricketer. Has again and again proved essential to his side. Batting and bowling, good and accurate; fielding excellent.'

Liddell's main rival was his brother Rob. Devoted friends though they were, they competed against each other for sporting honours and together they dominated the school's sports in the 1917–18 season, as demonstrated by the following results:

Cross Country Run: 1st. R.V. Liddell. 2nd. E.H. Liddell
Long Jump: 1st. E.H. Liddell. 2nd. R.V. Liddell
High Jump: 1st. R.V. Liddell. 2nd. E.H. Liddell
100 yards: 1st. E.H. Liddell. 2nd. R.V. Liddell
Hurdle Race: 1st. R.V. Liddell. 2nd. E.H. Liddell
Quarter Mile: 1st. E.H. Liddell. 2nd. R.V. Liddell

Curiously, despite his popularity and sporting prowess, he was never Head Boy nor the recipient of the Baynard Prize, awarded annually to the boy considered to have contributed most to school life during the year, even though his brother received the award. So did A. Leslie Gracie, the great Scottish rugby international with whom Liddell forged an outstanding partnership on the rugby field for Eltham, Edinburgh University and Scotland. In fact, Gracie outshone Eric in just about every department, even sprinting. By way of explanation, D.P. Thompson, Liddell's friend and future biographer, maintained that Liddell was a late developer whose true qualities only emerged when he left the somewhat narrow and restricted life of Eltham College, an observation soon to be realised.

2

THE ROAD TO PARIS

Liddell left Eltham College in the spring of 1920, needing to pass his entrance exam in French to join his brother Rob – who was reading medicine – at Edinburgh University. That summer, his mother, sister and youngest brother Ernest arrived from China and the family rented a furnished house in Edinburgh while Eric crammed hard and successfully for his exam and worked as a farm labourer. In the autumn of 1920, he enrolled in a four-year BSc degree in Pure Science, taking classes at the University's Heriot Watt College and proving himself a conscientious student as his marks testify. In the 1920–21 session, he achieved 94 per cent in Inorganic Chemistry and 83 per cent in Mathematics. Even in the Olympic year his marks never fell below 68 per cent, which suggests that he did not neglect his studies.

It was in the more cosmopolitan and competitive environment of university that Liddell's athletic career began in earnest; before that, he considered running as more of a recreational activity. At first, he declined offers to run by the University Athletics Club, citing too much academic work. However, the lure of the track proved to be too strong and he was soon back at training, entering for the University Sports in May 1921. Before that, however, much to the chagrin of his trainer, he set off for a cycling holiday on Ben Nevis (Britain's highest mountain) with four friends.

'I was only a novice then, and a novice was my trainer,' wrote Liddell. 'Both of us knowing very little or nothing about it, we got on extremely well together for the first week. Then came the holidays. I had made arrangements for a week's cycling tour. My novice friend said that that was the very worst thing for training. But all he said slid off my back like water off a duck's, for, after all, at that stage we were both novices, and I was quite sure that I knew as much about it as he did. Leaving him with his thoughts, I went off with four other friends for a cycle run to Ben Nevis. It took us exactly six days, from Monday morning to late on Saturday night. All of us agreed that it was a great success, despite the fact that when we reached the top of Ben Nevis at six o'clock one morning, and waited for the sun to rise, we found that that was one of the days on which the sun did not rise.

'Arriving back, I went to see if I would be able to run, but, alas! What I had been told was only too true. I was stiff, and there was no spring in my muscles, and only three or four more weeks before I was to make my first appearance in public as a runner.'

Fortunately, the 'springiness' returned to Liddell's legs and he was able to compete at the meeting. The University Sports marked Liddell's first public appearance as a runner and his debut was impressive indeed. He won the 100 yards (91.44 metres), beating the favourite, G. Innes-Stewart, by centimetres, and then came second in the 220 yards (201 metres) to the same runner. The latter race was the only time that Liddell ever lost a race in Scotland.

Now that he had demonstrated his calibre as a sprinter and was selected for the Inter-University Sports, he decided to take training more seriously and was taken to a track at the Powderhall Stadium, renowned for its dog racing. The experience proved to be illuminating, if not embarrassing, for Liddell. 'It was the first time in my life I had ever seen a cinder track.

'Many who trained there were professionals. Up to then I thought all professional runners would be first-class runners. They danced about on their toes as if they were stepping on hot bricks. Whenever they started to run, they dug big holes for their toes to go into, as if they were preparing for the time when their toes would dance no more. Surely they did not expect me to make such a fool of myself as all that? Yes, I found that they did.'

It was at Powderhall that Liddell met the experienced Tom McKerchar who became his new coach. McKerchar introduced him, much to his incredulity, to the finer points of training – warming-up, massage and specialist exercises for sprinters.

'He took me in hand, pounded me about like a piece of putty, pushed this muscle this way and that muscle the other way, in order, as he said, to get me into shape,' wrote Liddell of the experience.

'He told me that my muscles were all far too hard and that they needed to be softened by massage. He added that if they were not softened soon, some day when I tried to start, one of the muscles would snap. He took me out and told me to do a short run. After finishing the run I stopped more quickly than any of the others. When I asked him what he thought of it, he answered that if I wanted a breakdown I was going about it in the best possible manner, for it appears that one must never stop abruptly on reaching the tape.

'Thus, being thoroughly humiliated, feeling that my reputation had been dragged through the mud, that my self-respect was still wallowing in the mire, and that if I didn't get into the clutches of a trainer soon, every muscle in my body would give way and I should remain a physical wreck till the end of my days – I was then in a fit mental condition to start an athletic career.'

The relationship which grew between athlete and trainer was one of mutual respect, but both being laconic, little was spoken. After a training session Liddell would return to Powderhall Stadium's pavilion, strip and lie on a table, and his trainer would massage him systematically in silence. Liddell was later to acknowledge the debt he owed to McKerchar for getting him into shape, and no doubt in his own way, his trainer felt great pride that his man fulfilled his potential.

Two or three times a week Liddell could be seen down at the Powderhall track, limbering up and practising starts and sprints with a host of other sprinters in knee-length shorts on one side of the track, while whippets, straining their leashes and barking continuously, were on the other. There were no tracksuits or windcheaters in the twenties; on cold and windy days the athletes would remain in the pavilion until the last minute before emerging to race, an overcoat the only protection for their bare legs. Although Liddell stuck doggedly to his fitness regime, he never took naturally to training and had problems with his start which would continue to frustrate him throughout his athletic career.

'Training is not the easiest thing to do,' he once explained to a sports journalist. 'It is liable to become monotonous, with the continual repetition of certain exercises. One of the hardest lessons to learn is how to start. Time after time you go to your holes, rise to the "get set" position, and wait for the pistol to go. Someone tries to go off before the pistol, and so we all have to get up and start from the beginning again. Even after I had been at it for four years, the papers now and then reminded me that my weak point was the slowness with which I started.'

One of his closest and oldest friends, A.P. Cullen, who was one of his tutors at Eltham College and later a colleague, was convinced that Liddell's conscience would never allow him to 'beat the gun'. Whatever reservations Liddell had about training, his success on the track continued. He entered his first major competition, the Scottish Championships in 1921, with great expectations and, not unsurprisingly, great excitement.

'At last, the day dawned,' wrote Liddell. 'Needless to say I was excited. Excited is a very mild word to use in order to try to explain the various emotional tremors that vibrated through my system. My dinner that day was not a success, in fact it was a nasty failure. The food would not slide down the alimentary canal with any degree of ease, and any that did manage to get down hadn't a dog's chance of being digested. This is an experience that most athletes go through some time in their career, and it makes you ask yourself if it is all worth it.'

Undoubtedly it was, for Liddell overcame his nerves to win the 100 and 220 yards, titles he retained for the next four years. Not long after, he achieved his first international success when he won the 100 yards in a meeting between England, Ireland and Scotland held in Belfast. In 1923, he won both sprints and the quarter-mile in the same event.

As well as earning a reputation as a fine sprinter with world-class potential, Liddell won the enduring admiration and affection of both the spectators who faithfully attended the meetings in which he ran and his fellow competitors.

Professor Neil Campbell was an undergraduate with Liddell at Edinburgh University and has never forgotten the day he ran against him. 'There were no lanes in those days, just staggered starts, and he drew the inside lane and I drew the outside lane. He must have taken pity on me because he came up just before the race and said very quietly, "Let's swap places."'

Such was the influence that Liddell had on Campbell that the latter was to remark later, 'No athlete has ever made a bigger impact on people all over the world, and the description of him as "the most famous, the most popular, and the best-loved athlete Scotland has ever produced" is no exaggeration.'

One athlete recalls Liddell digging his starting holes with a trowel and then graciously offering his opponents the use of it; most gratefully accepted it. With a delightful smile, he approached each athlete in turn and shook his hand. He then got 'on his marks' with them, was off at the gun, and won a very fine race from the outside berth.

A spectator at a University Sports meeting in Edinburgh remembers observing a black student wandering about, awaiting his event. 'Not a single person was speaking to him. He seemed so much alone and my heart went out to him, so much so that I felt like going to talk to him myself. To my great joy, Eric went up to him, put his arm in his and engaged him in friendly conversation until his event. It was, I thought, such a beautiful Christian action and it has lived in my memory ever since.'

A student from a Scottish university recalls another act of kindness typical of Liddell. 'Eric Liddell, whom I had met and competed against the year before at St Andrews, was an Edinburgh competitor, and I was representing Aberdeen. Towards the end of the Sports I was, rather thoughtlessly, sitting on the cold turf wearing nothing but a light singlet, shorts and spiked shoes, and waiting for the last event of the afternoon to start. Liddell, strolling in my direction, saw me sitting and, to my surprise, took off his Edinburgh blue blazer and placed it over my shoulders to keep me warm. He did this with a smile and a word of advice about avoiding the cold. A small enough gesture, it might be said, but a spontaneous Christ-like one towards one who was virtually a stranger from another Varsity. I have never forgotten this kindly act, and not by any means only because Eric Liddell afterwards became so famous.'

In his first year at Edinburgh University, Liddell emerged as its star athlete just as he had done at Eltham College, but rugby was his passion and the University selectors were not slow to appreciate his talent. By his second year at Edinburgh, Liddell was playing for the University First XV in which he renewed his successful 'wing' partnership with A. Leslie Gracie.

Impressive in subsequent trials for Scotland, Liddell made his international debut on 2 January 1922 against France in Paris. Although not outstanding in this game, he proved his mettle a few weeks later in a 'final' trial.

'Of the eight three-quarters,' declared *The Scotsman*, 'only E.H. Liddell was really satisfactory. Great speed, sure hands, and the ability to turn opponents' failings to account marked his work. The only thrills came from him. He was the only player with the hallmark "international" stamped on him.'

In his second season Liddell matured into an indispensable member of the Scottish team. The combination of Gracie's skill and elusiveness and Liddell's pace secured Scotland's first victory over Wales at the Arms Park in Cardiff since 1890. As a testament to the magnitude of their contribution to this famous victory, Liddell and Gracie were carried off the field by the defeated Welsh team.

The Scotsman reported the following of the duo's performance:

> Gracie was the vital, living force in the three-quarter line. His partner on the wing, E.H. Liddell, improves with every game he plays. He runs now with more determination than he showed last year, and he showed real grit and some football on several occasions. Had he a less extraordinary man beside him, he might be much more dangerous than he is ever allowed to be.

Weeks later, Scotland triumphed again, this time over Ireland, at thirteen points to three. 'It was entirely due to a clever move by Liddell,' commented *The Scotsman* again on the first half of the game, 'that the Scots owed their lead.' It was again due to Liddell that Scotland went further ahead.

Only in the last match of the season – the Calcutta Cup against England – did Scotland lose by two points and this had nothing to do with Liddell, who was presented with few chances to turn the match. It proved to be Eric Liddell's last international for Scotland – from then on he decided to concentrate fully on running – and the end of a brief but promising career as a rugby player.

Whether Liddell had the ability to be a rugby great is a matter of conjecture. The Scottish sporting journalist, William Reid, contended that, 'Liddell liked running but he loved football. For all that, he is not a natural footballer, as he is a natural runner, and although he was too plucky and too good a tackier to be stigmatised as a "mere sprinter", he had not the attributes, the knack and the craft of the great footballer.'

As the 1923 athletics season opened, Liddell, despite his track successes in Scotland, had still not competed in London and his chances of being selected for the British Olympic team were not considered promising, even in his native Scotland. This perception was reinforced by his performances in that year's Scottish Amateur Athletic Championships in Glasgow. Although he won the 100 and 220 yards as expected, his times did not live up to expectations.

Even Liddell himself, remarkable as it now seems in retrospect, considered it a waste of £5 for the Scottish Amateur Athletics Association to send him to Stamford Bridge in London to compete in the British Championships, due to his apparent loss of form. One can only speculate whether Liddell would have made the Olympic team if he had not competed that day, for he ran like a man inspired.

The British Championships opened on 6 July in sweltering heat – loosening muscles and thus perfect weather for sprinters, but the schedules did not bode well for Liddell. He discovered that he had to run twice on the Friday in the preliminary heats of the 100 and 220 yards. Then four times the next day in the second round of the heats at 2.30 and 3.10 p.m. and then in the finals at 3.40 and 4.50 p.m. Defying his recent poor form, he won all six races and in the final of the 100 yards he ran the race of his life, bursting through the tape after recovering from his usual poor start, in a new British record of 9.7 seconds (one of the longest-standing British athletics records and not surpassed until Peter Radford clocked 9.6 seconds in 1958). In the 220 yards he recorded a personal best of 21.6 seconds and for this outstanding dual performance he was awarded the Harvey Cup as Best Athlete of the Year. But most important of all, his victories in the sprints clinched his place in the British

Olympic team and established him as a world-class athlete and Britain's best hope for a gold medal in the 100 metres, an accolade that was later to weigh heavily upon him.

If there were any doubts that Liddell's performance at Stamford Bridge was just a freak occurrence, then they were soon dispelled when he single-handedly secured victory for Scotland in a competition against England and Ireland by winning the 100, 220 and 440 yards (402 metres). His win in the 440 yards was particularly impressive considering that he had done no training and had virtually no experience at the distance. The race proved to be one of the most remarkable ever run by an athlete. As *The Scotsman* remarked, 'The circumstances in which he won made it a performance bordering on the miraculous.'

The runners were started on the bend, Liddell having the inside berth, but the Scot had taken only three strides when Gillies (England) crashed into him and knocked him off the track. He stumbled on the grass, and for a moment seemed half inclined to give it up. Then suddenly he sprang forward and was after his opponents like a flash.

By this time the leaders were about twenty yards ahead, but Liddell gradually drew up on them, and by the time the home stretch was reached he was running fourth. He would have to be about ten yards behind Gillies then. It seemed out of the question that he could win, but he achieved the apparently impossible. Forty yards from home he was third, and seemed on the point of collapsing, but pulling himself together he put in a desperate finish to win by two yards from Gillies.

One of Liddell's team mates who witnessed his collapse as he broke the tape wrote, 'When he collapsed I was one of those who helped him to the pavilion, and on the suggestion of a drop of brandy to revive him, he semi-consciously remarked to me, "No thanks, Jimmy, just a drop of strong tea."'

The *Peking and Tientsin Times'* report of Liddell's heroic victory was even more dramatic than *The Scotsman's*. 'Eric,' it stated with understandable hyperbole, 'was unconscious for over half-an-hour. The muscles in the thigh stiffened, and the nerves in his head became affected. But he soon recovered.'

By modern standards, Liddell had an appalling style of running. Nearly always off to a bad start, his body swayed as he brought his knees up very high, head thrust back, mouth open and fists punching the air. 'A curious action,' remarked old opponent Innes-Stewart somewhat understatedly. Yet that extraordinary technique somehow propelled him towards the finishing line faster than anyone else in the country, if not the world.

Liddell's eccentric style of running also intrigued his wife Florence. 'The way he threw his head back – it was so ridiculous! Boy I couldn't understand how he could ever see. When I asked him he just said, "I knew where I was going all right."'

Fellow student athlete, Neil Campbell, is convinced that, despite having his head back, Liddell could still see where he was going. However, an incident that occurred when Liddell was running the 100 metres solo in China in 1929 suggests that when the head went back he really was trusting in God to guide him to the finishing line. Annie Buchan, matron of the mission hospital in Xiaochang, where Liddell would one day be based as an itinerant evangelist, recalled what happened:

'I will never forget Eric coming along with his head back and tearing along. A Chinese photographer, not realising the speed he was travelling at, came right into

Eric's path with his tripod. Of course Eric came right into him. The photographer went flying and the tripod too, and Eric fell flat on his face. Rob [Liddell's brother] and I rushed down. Eric was just lying there, and we carried him into a tent unconscious. And when he came round, do you know what he said? "I was just winded."'

Harold Abrahams, Liddell's sprint rival and the 1924 Olympic 100 metres gold medallist, remarked in 1934 about Liddell: 'No runner of his superb ability ever possessed a worse style. It was unorthodox in the extreme. Head back, arms all over the place and an exaggerated knee drive, there was hardly anything about his movements that would commend itself to the experienced onlooker. Indeed, my reaction on seeing him perform for the first time (in a heat of the 220 yards at the AAA Championships in 1923) was that I was witnessing the most misplaced direction of great energy I had ever imagined possible. I realised his power to the full when I had a back view of him in the semi-final of that 220 yards later that evening.'

His awkward style caused problems for Ian Charleson, who played Liddell in the film *Chariots of Fire*. Running with his head back, Charleson couldn't see where he was going and kept veering off the track or colliding with other athletes. Then he recalled his drama school 'trust' exercises, when he had been urged to run as hard as possible towards a wall and trust that someone would catch him. He realised that was how Liddell must have run, with his head up; he literally trusted to get there.

Tom McNab, a British National Coach between 1963 and 1977, was hired by the producers of *Chariots of Fire* to teach Charleson how to mimic Liddell's ungainly running style. According to McNab, by today's standards Liddell would have been a consummate athlete and may even have made the finals of the Olympics or World Athletics Championships but would not have been good enough to win a gold medal, particularly in the 400 metres. Contends McNab, Liddell, at only 5 feet 9 inches (1.75 metres) tall, would be limited by his size and his real potential would have been in the 100 metres, not the 400.

McNab also points out that although Liddell's times were remarkable for the amount of training he put in, they have to be put in perspective. Very few people ran competitively in the twenties and thirties and those who did were usually the privileged few – including Eric Liddell – who attended public schools and went to university. Astonishingly, 20 per cent of the 1924 British Olympic team were attending the universities of Oxford and Cambridge. The vast majority of the British population never had the time, money nor access to facilities to enable them to pursue a career in athletics.

According to Neil Campbell, Liddell would never have been prepared to put in the commitment required by today's athletes to reach the top. 'If he was around today? He'd still have been a splendid runner, but I don't think he'd have been able to participate in all the big championships here, there and everywhere. I just don't think he would have done it. You see, training in those days wasn't anything like we do now. A seven-day week training session was just not on for him. He had his studies and other commitments. His training was fairly intensive – but only two or three times a week. There was nothing like the fantastic dedication of today – that just wasn't on. Eric's studies – although he wasn't a particularly great student – were essential to him and he had to get a degree. Running was important – he got a great deal of pleasure out of it – but it took second place.'

Liddell was very much the gentleman amateur, as the majority of athletes were in the twenties. 'Eric would turn in his grave if he saw the way today's athletes run around with the name of commercial advertisers emblazoned on their gear,' asserts Tom Riddell, former Scottish champion miler and Liddell contemporary. 'He'd have been appalled at the sight of "amateurs" running for money. And as for those fellows who do a lap of honour after winning!'

A modern athlete's diet, full of supplements and vitamin pills, would probably shock Liddell too. He ate whatever his companions did when he was staying at the Edinburgh Medical Missionary Society hostel in George Square. His only concession was on the day of a race, when he avoided heavy, fatty foods, although he once ate plum pudding and ran his second-fastest 440 yards ever in Scotland.

McNab suggests that Liddell's attitude to running was more casual, more cavalier than that of contemporary athletes. A top sprinter today could not get away with two or three days' training a week or consuming whatever food was put in front of him as Liddell did. But for all that, Liddell was committed to his running and to winning. His training schedule may not have been as intensive as a modern athlete's, but he had no less a burning desire for victory. What else could have driven him to the point of exhaustion and unconsciousness to win a race after losing nearly twenty metres?

But was the ambition to be the best in the world all that inspired this quiet, unassuming university student to reach such exalted heights of athletic achievement? 'To mount with wings as eagles,' to quote one of Liddell's favourite scriptures. Or, when the head went back and the mouth opened, did running become a highly charged spiritual experience?

3

IN SEARCH OF PERFECTION

Despite his dazzling success on the running track and meteoric rise to national prominence Eric Liddell remained modest and unaffected. The Edinburgh University magazine, *The Student*, wrote in December 1923: 'Ninety-nine men gifted with Eric's prowess would now be insufferably swollen-headed, but here we have the hundredth man. Here is a man who hates praise and shuns publicity, yet is deserving of both.' Once, when asked by a fellow athlete how he overcame the temptations of egotism and conceit, Liddell replied with typical laconicism and simplicity, 'I prayed about it.'

If not kudos and acclaim, then what was the source of Liddell's astonishing drive to win, to push himself to the very limit of his endurance to the point of exhaustion and beyond? Someone who once asked how he so often managed to snatch victory from the jaws of defeat with one last all-consuming effort received the reply, 'The fact is, I don't like to be beaten.'

Not even it seems by a bus! When out training one day in Edinburgh with a group of running mates, a bus drew up and honked a challenge. Only Liddell had the energy and determination to race after the bus and just beat it to the top of the hill. 'I just don't like to be beaten,' he exclaimed, gasping for breath, to his friends when they eventually caught up with him.

Yet within Eric Liddell, there lay an even greater force that drove him on in the pursuit of excellence, to attain a state of perfection in whatever he set out to accomplish, whether it were racing a bus, competing for an Olympic gold medal or in the everyday mundanities of life. Following Liddell's death the Reverend T.T. Faichney, who was minister at the Union Church in Tianjin (formerly Tientsin) which Liddell attended and where he was married in the 1930s, said, 'Everything that Eric did, he did well; he had a passion for perfection. For one who was among the world's fleetest of foot, I often marvelled that he was so slow in speech and in the things he did. But it was because nothing less than the best was good enough.'

'Whenever I think of Eric, one picture comes into my mind, which I think typifies my experience of living with him,' wrote Dr George Dorling, who shared a flat with Liddell in Tianjin during the late twenties and early thirties. 'He came into my room with his blue eyes very bright, as if he had just discovered some new secret. In his hand was a New Testament. "Look George," he said, and drew my attention to this verse. "'Be ye perfect.' He said it and he means it," said Eric. "You and I can and should be no less than that – perfect, even as our Heavenly Father is."

'Eric lived up to that. That was the standard by which he judged his actions. Whenever he fell short of this perfect life – and he weighed his actions, words and thoughts in this balance before God each morning in his quiet time – whenever he had not attained that perfection which Jesus commanded, then he recognised it as sin and took appropriate steps to put it right.'

The most famous, the most popular and the best-loved athlete Scotland has ever produced.

Eric Liddell was 'more than an athlete', and the stand he took in 1924 against competing on a Sunday, together with his decision to forsake fame and fortune to go to China as a missionary, caught the imagination of a generation.

The Liddell children in 1914. Eric is on the right beside Ernest, with Rob and Jenny on the left.

When their missionary parents returned to China in 1908, Rob and Eric went to Eltham College in Kent.

At Eltham Eric and Rob excelled in many sports. The
1917 1st Cricket XI. They are middle left.

They were also successively captains of the 1st XV
rugby teams, Eric in 1918.

In 1922 Eric gained the first of his seven international rugby caps. He is at the front on the right.

Eric created his first Scottish track record over 220 yards at the University Sports at Craiglockhart in 1922.

This was the secret of Eric Liddell's success on the running track: to glorify God by striving for perfection without compromise. That is not to say that Liddell's creed was to win at all costs. Running exhilarated him and he loved to win, to prove he was the best in his event, but he never sought personal glory nor revelled in his exceptional athletic ability. Magnanimous in defeat, he had no lust for victory. When a friend asked him whether he ever prayed that he would win a race, Liddell replied characteristically, 'No, I have never prayed that I would win a race. I have, of course, prayed about the athletic meetings, asking that in this too, God might be glorified.'

Liddell believed in the saving power of the Crucifixion; that the Bible is the literal word of God; that obedience to God and the surrendering of one's will to the Lord's are essential prerequisites for a successful Christian life. 'He was literally,' claimed A.P. Cullen, 'God-controlled, in his thoughts, judgements, actions, words, to an extent I have never seen surpassed, and rarely seen equalled.'

As Liddell asserts in his *Manual for the Christian Disciple*, written in 1942:

> Obedience to God's will is the secret of spiritual knowledge and insight . . . Let us put ourselves before ourselves and look at ourselves. The bravest moment in a man's life is the moment he looks at himself objectively without wincing, without complaining. Self-examination which does not result in action is dangerous. What am I going to do about what I see? The action called for is surrender to God.

Cullen often heard him utter the words 'absolute surrender'. The concept was always in his mind that God should have absolute control over every part of his life.

'It was towards the attainment of that ideal that he directed all his mental and spiritual energies. It was no more easy for him than it is for us; let no one think that he did not have his temptations, just as we have, temptations to indolence, slackness, compromise and what not. But he won his way through, by persistent study, regular times of devotion, constant meditation, insistent prayer, getting up early in the morning and spending one hour – two hours – in a concentrated search for God's will as revealed in the teaching of Jesus and the Bible generally.'

The early morning appointments with God were the source of Liddell's spiritual strength and consistency, and throughout the rest of his life he rarely missed one. Dr Kenneth McAll who worked as a surgeon at the mission hospital in north China in the late 1930s where Liddell was an evangelist, remembers the times they used to pray together silently in the mornings. 'Those early morning "quiet times" were the key to everything,' explained McAll. 'We would sit for about an hour, listening as well as talking to God. There was complete silence, and often we were both smiling as if at a private joke.'

'What was his secret?' wrote an internee of the Japanese internment camp in China where Liddell spent the last two years of his life. 'Once I asked him, but I really knew already, for my husband was in his dormitory and shared the secret with him. Every morning about 6 a.m., with curtains tightly drawn to keep in the shining of their peanut-oil lamp, lest the prowling sentries should think someone was trying to escape, he used to climb out of his top bunk, past the sleeping forms of his dormitory mates. Then, at the small Chinese table, the two men would sit close together with the light just enough to illuminate their Bibles and notebooks. Silently, they read, prayed, thought about the day's duties, noted what should be done.

'Eric was a man of prayer, not only at set times – though he did not like to miss a Prayer Meeting or Communion Service, when such could be arranged. He talked to God all the time, naturally, as one can who enters the "School of Prayer" to learn this way of inner discipline.'

Liddell appears to have been influenced by the Oxford Group, an evangelistic movement established in 1918 by the American evangelist Frank Buchman (who later became involved in the more politically motivated 'Moral Rearmament'), and which flourished in the twenties and thirties. A member had to confess and repent of his sins, accept Jesus Christ as his Saviour, and publicly share his faith. Integral to its creed were the four moral absolutes of honesty, purity, unselfishness and love.

Although there is no clear evidence to prove that Liddell was a member, he did attend a number of meetings and house parties organised by the Group, and offered it a glowing tribute in 1932. 'The Group has brought to me personally a greater power in my life, discipline without the thought of discipline, and a greater willingness to share the deepest things in my life. In my time in this country, I have met no body of people who are so vitally active and through whom the Spirit of God works so clearly as the Oxford Group.'

Liddell was no spiritual elitist; he did not impose his faith on others nor did he point an accusing finger at those who failed to emulate his exalted standards. A close friend wrote, 'I never heard Eric say an unkind word of anyone. I often heard him point out the spark of good in people others thought were hopeless. "Yes, but what a wonderful Christian he would make," he would say.'

Love and compassion, epitomised by one of Liddell's favourite biblical verses, Paul's exaltation of love in his first letter to the Corinthians, took precedence over rigid theological doctrine. Wrote Cullen, 'To him the supreme thing about God was God's love, even as love is the supreme necessity for a truly Christian life.' A love demonstrated on many occasions to George Dorling and his flatmates in Tianjin: 'We three were miles below the standard Eric set for himself. But he was always our friend. I knew that every time I could count on Eric. Nothing ever shocked him. His love was too great to be shocked – it was like God's.'

And there was always that quiet smile, those twinkling blue eyes and gentle sense of humour to temper any quarrel or petty difference in religious opinion.

Mary Hamilton remembered when Liddell was secretary of the Young People's Union at Edinburgh's Morningside Church (now the Eric Liddell Centre). She still treasures the invitation card, which reads:

> Mary, who chose the better part
> We are trying our simple art
> And if by chance we entice you to
> The precincts of the YPU
> This coming Tuesday is the date
> Come at thirty minutes to eight.

At the party, a game was played which involved 'fishing' with a string and bent pin for packages of sandwiches and buns. Eric 'caught' one, then surreptitiously blew up the empty bag and put it back. He did not know he had been seen until Mary gave her account of the hoax at a subsequent gathering. 'Wherever Eric was, there was laughter,' she recalled. 'He had such a lovely, quiet sense of humour.'

'The thing that struck me most about Eric,' remarked his wife Florence, 'was his sense of humour. It used to stagger me the way people would disagree violently with him and say the bitterest things, but Eric would just smile and pass it off in his quiet way. I think it was because in his heart he felt he was right and he felt that nothing was ever accomplished by losing one's temper.

'Eric wasn't at all holy, holy. His wonderful sense of humour saved him from ever being like that. He had a poker-faced humour, and you had to watch his eyes very carefully. They usually gave him away, if you looked closely.'

Liddell's desire to glorify God through his running became an even greater conviction after his public confession of his faith. D.P. Thompson was convinced that after this disclosure his sprinting was 'more brilliant than ever', concluding that, 'spiritual liberation has as profound an effect on a man's mind and body as it has on his soul'. Was it a coincidence that Liddell broke the British record for the 100 yards soon after his 'confession'?

Certainly his old friend A.P. Cullen believed it was the Holy Spirit within which elevated him from being just good to the ranks of the exceptional, when he remarked twenty years later, 'Eric is the most remarkable example of a man of average ability and talents developing those talents to an amazing degree, and even appearing to acquire new talents from time to time, through the power of the Holy Spirit.'

Thompson describes Liddell's public declaration of his Christianity as 'perhaps the first great spiritual crisis of his life'. With missionaries as parents, Liddell had an upbringing steeped in the principles of the Christian faith. At Eltham College, he regularly attended the weekly Bible class, although he shied away from discussions.

At the age of 15, he became a full member of his church in Edinburgh, assisted in forming a branch of the Crusaders' Union at school and was involved in the Islington Medical Mission. However, 'To his own great impoverishment as well as to that of others,' suggests Thompson, 'he had been a secret disciple. Of his influence for good there could be no question – it was acknowledged on every hand – but he had never disclosed his secret and had never openly confessed his Lord.'

In the spring of 1923, Liddell, by this time a famous athlete in Scotland, was invited by Thompson to speak at an evangelistic meeting in the industrial town of Armadale in central Scotland. The meeting was one of a series organised by the Glasgow Students' Evangelistic Union – an interdenominational group of which Rob, Liddell's brother, was an active member – dedicated to evangelising that region of Scotland. 'I put the proposition to him as directly and as forcibly as I could,' recalled Thompson. 'There was a moment's silence while Eric dropped his head to consider. Then came the answer in the friendly tone I was to know so well, "All right. I'll come!"'

The evangelistic meeting at Armadale Town Hall was not particularly well attended considering Liddell's celebrity status – only about seventy to eighty men turned up to hear him speak. There was no slick presentation or emotional appeals for money that often characterises contemporary evangelism. There was no mesmeric, hysteria-inducing oratory either. Diffident and shy, he proved to be a mediocre speaker. Public speaking was a nerve-wracking experience for Liddell, as it was for his brother Rob. Yet those who attended that night listened with rapt attention as numerous audiences would in the years to come, drawn not by gimmicks, but by the power of his personality, the conviction of his beliefs and the way he could relate to the problems they faced daily.

'He was no great orator by any means,' recalled former Lutheran missionary Marcy Ditmanson, who listened to Liddell preach while they were both interned in a Japanese prison camp in China. 'But he had a way of riveting his listeners with those marvellous, clear blue eyes of his. Yes, that's what I remember most about him as he spoke – those wonderful eyes and how they would twinkle.'

Ian Charleson became aware of how much this ordinary, down-to-earth quality that Liddell possessed contributed to his appeal when he was researching the role of Liddell for *Chariots of Fire*. 'The way I see it, he never pushed his faith down anyone's throat. When he spoke, he spoke rather quietly. He just talked about real things – about himself and his faith and what he did that morning.'

Lord David Puttnam, producer of *Chariots of Fire*, vividly recalls a remark made by Eric's widow Florence when she first saw the film. 'You know your wee man [Charleson], he did something Eric could never have done for himself,' referring to the eloquence in which Charleson delivered his lines. 'Eric wasn't a good speaker. He had a real problem with crowds and getting his deep conviction across to large groups of people. He knew it and regretted it.'

Liddell's decision to speak at Armadale proved to be a turning point in his life. He would never again refuse an invitation to speak of his faith unless it was physically impossible to fit the engagement in. More than a decade later in Tianjin, China, where he was a college tutor, one of his flatmates observed, 'Eric made it a rule that he never refused to speak for his Lord if it was physically possible to fit in the engagement. The result was that often he would have four or even five services in a day, going from one to the other. But he never let it worry him. He just spoke simply – usually on what God had revealed to him that morning.'

The path Eric Liddell was to follow undeviatingly from now on and for the rest of his life, a direction, contended Thompson, that had already been decided upon at school, had been confirmed – the complete surrender of his will to God. And the determination to pursue this principle without compromise would soon cost Liddell the chance of winning an Olympic gold medal and arouse the wrath of a nation.

4

THE ONLY THING IN LIFE THAT MATTERS?

When the timetables for the Olympic Games were released in November 1923 and it was revealed that the heats of the 100 metres were scheduled for a Sunday, Eric Liddell immediately withdrew from the event and from the 4 × 100 and 4 × 400 relays, whose heats were also on a Sunday. Liddell's determination to observe the Sabbath as a day of rest dedicated to God shocked both the British athletics fraternity and the public. Here was one of the world's top sprinters who had recently come within a tenth of a second of the world record for the 100 yards, throwing away the chance of winning a gold medal in the blue ribbon event of the Games because of a religious principle.

'It was all very quiet,' remembers fellow athlete, Neil Campbell. 'Liddell was the last person to make a song and dance about that sort of thing. He just said, "I'm not running on a Sunday" – and that was that! And he would have been upset if anything much had been made of it at the time. We thought it was completely in character, and a lot of the athletes were quietly impressed by it. They felt that here was a man who was prepared to stand for what he thought was right, without interfering with anyone else, and without being dogmatic or anything like that.'

'He didn't take us by surprise because we knew his feelings about games on Sunday,' recalls Greville Young, one of the students who shared a hostel in George Square, Edinburgh with Liddell. 'But it caused a tremendous furore among many people, particularly the newspapers. I remember how they came to the George Square hostel and hammered on the door and demanded to see him. On one occasion, it was my job to go down and try and clear them off. They were quite menacing. There were cries of, "He's a traitor to his country!"'

Dr George Graham-Cummings, another student who lodged at the George Square hostel, raced and wrestled with Liddell whom he remembers as being very burly with a deep chest and enormous vital capacity. 'Running with us in the Gardens was really a good-natured joke on his part. I'd been considered pretty fast myself at school, but he gave me five yards' start in the 100 yards dash, waited until I'd taken off at full speed, then ran after me to pace me until the seventy-five yard mark and then just vanished in smoke thereafter. He was a man very easy to love, but would most certainly not have welcomed any too obvious demonstration of adoration.

'Not long before the Olympics, I almost lamed him by putting too vigorous a judo leg lock on him. That taught me what being unpopular with the British public can mean, but shortly thereafter, Eric refused to race on a Sunday and became the most unpopular man in Britain.'

Liddell was now entered only for the 200 metres, but there was still time for him to train for the 400, which he duly entered a month later in December. His remarkable victory at the Triangular meeting between England,

Scotland and Ireland had demonstrated his potential in the event, but he had never considered it his 'natural' distance. Recalled Florence, 'Eric always said that the great thing for him was that when he stood by his principles and refused to run in the 100 metres, he found that the 400 metres was really his race. He said he would never have known that otherwise. He would never have dreamed of trying the 400 at the Olympics.'

The 1924 athletic season commenced for Liddell in April with a trip to the United States to compete in a series of sprints at Pennsylvania University. In the 100 yards he finished fourth behind top American sprinter, Chester Bowman, with only 30 inches (76 centimetres) separating the first four runners. In the 220 yards, he was narrowly beaten again by another American, L.A. Clarke, who won in a time of 21.6 seconds.

Sir Arthur Marshall was a member of a Cambridge University athletics team invited to run at the Pennsylvania University meeting. During the ten-day return voyage aboard the SS *Republic* he struck up a friendship with Liddell and they played cards to while away the time. They also met two young American girls – Freddy and Edith – who were planning to see Europe. 'They said they'd be in Paris for the Games and if Eric and I were picked for the team we could perhaps meet up,' recalls Marshall. 'Well, he was of course and we did – we took them to a tea dance on the Champs-Elysées. I know it's hard to envisage the great Olympic hero and man of God doing the Charleston, but he did and with great gusto. He was tremendous fun, not at all a prig and he never talked religion.'

The Paris Olympics opened on Saturday 5 July 1924, in sweltering heat with temperatures reaching 45 °C. Some described the Colombes Stadium as a cauldron, others as a furnace and one of the refreshment stalls was humourously dubbed *La Bonne Frite* ('The Good Fry').

Three thousand competitors from forty-four nations (15 more than in Antwerp in 1920) had entered for the Games, with the Americans with 400 participants having the largest contingent.

In charge of ensuring that the British athletes got to the stadium on time for their events was Captain (later General and Sir) Philip Christison of the 2nd Queen's Own Cameron Highlanders, who were to provide the official British musicians for the Games. The task was complicated by the wealthy American team which had established a virtual monopoly on Parisian taxis by offering outrageously high fares. Christison was often forced to resorting to flagging down private vehicles in the street in order to get the British athletes to the stadium.

In his capacity as a minder, Christison had ample opportunity to chat with the athletes, including Liddell, who was still being pressured by British athletic officials and the press to change his mind and run in the heats of the 100 metres. Recalls Christison, 'He said to me once, "I wonder if I'm doing the right thing." But he added a minute later, "Yes, I'm sure I'm right."' Christison himself once attempted to get Liddell to change his mind and received the somewhat terse reply, 'Don't pressure me. I've made up my mind. I'm not going to run on the Lord's day and that's that!'

Liddell was reminded yet again of his 'betrayal' when one of the British dignitaries at the Games, Lord Cadogan, remarked pointedly to an assembled British team, including Liddell, 'To play the game is the only thing in life that matters.' The Scotsman chipped in with its own nationalistic comment, stating that, 'The British team will play the game, thus upholding the honour and reputation of Great Britain.' For most, it seemed, despite the horrendous sacrifices made during the First World War, King and country still came a long way before God.

On Tuesday 8 July, the day after he watched Harold Abrahams win the 100 metres in a personal best of 10.6 seconds, the first European to do so, Liddell sailed through his heats of the 200 metres. In the final the following day, he was pitted against Jackson Scholz, runner-up in the 100 metres, Charles Paddock, the world record holder, and Abrahams. Scholz stormed through to win in 21.6 seconds, with Paddock second and Liddell third. Abrahams trailed in sixth and last.

Finishing third was no mean achievement, although some thought he could have done better, noting that he failed to produce his usual Herculean finish. *The Scotman*'s report of Liddell's bronze was subdued to say the least, neglecting to mention that it was the first time a Scot had won a medal in the 200 metres. 'Eric Liddell, the Scottish sprinter, scored points for Britain by running into third place. He was well placed and had his spurt been forthcoming, he would undoubtedly have won.'

Perhaps the newspaper still had not forgiven him for withdrawing from the 100 metres. A more likely reason for such a paltry few lines on a medal-winning performance was that the Olympic Games did not carry the same status as they do today and were not deemed important enough to warrant extensive coverage, unless a British athlete won, of course.

Liddell's bid for the 400-metres crown opened on 10 July with a less than scintillating 50.2 seconds in the first round. Later in the day, he won his quarter-final heat in a personal best of 49.0 seconds, followed by 48.2 in the semi-final the next day. He appeared to be peaking at just the right time, but so were his rivals. Switzerland's

Joseph Imbach and Britain's Guy Butler had both broken the world record in earlier heats, a record which was shattered again soon after by Horatio Fitch of the United States with a scorching 47.8 seconds.

On the morning of the day of the final, Friday 11 July, Liddell received a note from the British team's masseur (not Jackson Scholz as *Chariots of Fire* implies) that read: 'In the old book it says: "He that honours me, I will honour" [referring to the biblical 1 Samuel 2:30 "Them that honour me I will honour"]. Wishing you the best of success always.' He revealed later that he wrote the note simply because he 'liked Eric so much'. In the dressing room after the race, as he lay on the treatment table, Liddell thanked the masseur. 'I did his left side and I remember what a great heart he had,' recalled the masseur. 'Eric Liddell had that sort of effect on people.'

As the six competitors lined up on the track for the final of the 400 metres on another blisteringly hot afternoon, few could have given the inexperienced Liddell much of a chance, especially as he had been drawn in the sixth and outside lane with no one to pace him and no idea of the progress of his rivals. Britain's hopes still rested with Guy Butler, silver medallist in the 400 at the 1920 Antwerp Games, despite his injured leg, which required a heavy bandage and forced him to start from a standing position.

As usual, Liddell shook hands with each of his opponents and then, minutes before the race was to start, the air was suddenly rent by the wail of bagpipes as the Cameron Highlanders struck up the rousing 'Scotland the Brave' as they marched round the Stadium. 'We just wanted to give Liddell a lift,' chuckled Christison. 'The atmosphere was so light-hearted that I said, "Come on, let's strike up" – and there was nothing the French could do to stop us.'

As the strains of the pipes faded away, a deathly hush descended on the stadium.

'To your marks!' cried the Olympic official.

Muscles tensed as the competitors awaited the report of the gun. Then suddenly, shattering the silence, the starting pistol cracked. Eric Liddell, in the outside lane, shot out of his starting holes as though he were running the 100-metres sprint. He stormed past the 200-metre mark in 22.2 seconds – only 0.6 of a second slower than Jackson Scholz's winning time in the 200-metres two days before. 'Surely he can't keep this pace up,' whispered people in the stand. 'He's bound to tie up in the home straight.'

Horatio Fitch, on paper the fastest man in the field, was in the lane next to Liddell. 'He set a terrific pace down the first stretch, but I matched his speed. He was only two yards ahead. I heard the other runners behind us. I knew the duel would be between the two of us,' recalled Fitch.

'Around the turn, he held the same pace. I couldn't believe a man could set such a pace and finish. The reporters expected the race to be between the Swiss [Imbach] and me because we had both broken the world's record. But Liddell pushed himself like a man possessed, head tilted back with determination.

'He was still two yards ahead when we entered the final turn. I knew I could close the gap. I had always had a good kick.

'The tape loomed 100 metres ahead. I pushed with everything I had, but Liddell fought to hold the advantage. Suddenly, behind us, Joseph Imbach snagged the string with his spikes and skidded to the track.

'I remembered what my coach had told me: "When you are getting tiredest, keep your arms driving high." I wasn't tired, but I couldn't go any faster. Every second,

I expected the Scot to slow down, to "tie up". He had sprinted the entire race, an unusual feat because most coaches believed then that a runner could not sprint 400 metres.

'Liddell didn't weaken. And we were closing on the tape much too quickly. I pulled closer, but he strained until we were again the same distance apart. With the tape only twenty metres away, I again spurted closer, but Liddell threw his head farther back, gathered himself together, and shot forward.' Liddell burst through the tape five metres ahead. His winning time – 47.6 seconds – was a new world and Olympic record.

'I went up to congratulate Liddell,' recalls Fitch, 'and he was pleasant, but rather aloof. I suppose that was the way most of the British were at the time. He never really said much of anything to me.'

The British newspapers, once notable for their understatement and the paucity of their coverage of the Games, now wrote with unrestrained enthusiasm. Clearly, all was forgiven: Eric Liddell had more than redeemed himself. Waxing lyrical, *The Scotsman* gushed:

> The Union Jack flew in proud majesty over Colombes Stadium today for the only Final down for decision, the 400 metres, which resulted in a great victory for Great Britain. The brilliant running of E.H. Liddell, the Edinburgh University sprinter, was responsible.
>
> There was gasp of astonishment when Eric Liddell, one of the most popular athletes at Colombes, was seen to be a clear three yards ahead of the field at the half distance. Nearing the tape, Fitch and Butler strained every nerve and muscle to overtake him, but could make absolutely no impression on the inspired Scot. With 20 yards to go, Fitch seemed to gain a fraction, Liddell appeared to sense the American, and with his head back

and chin thrust out in his usual style, he flashed past the tape to gain what was probably the greatest victory of the meeting so far. The crowd went into a frenzy of enthusiasm, which was renewed when the loudspeaker announced that once again the world's record had gone by the board.

The *Edinburgh Evening News* was even more effusive in its praise:

All round the banked area, people were on their feet cheering madly, and as if by magic, hosts of Union Jacks appeared above the heads of the raving crowd as Liddell ripped through the tape and into the arms of the Britishers who were waiting for him. For a moment the cheering lasted, then from the loudspeaker came: 'Hello, hello. Winner of the 400 metres: Liddell of Great Britain. The time 47.6 is a new world record.' Again, the great roar of cheering went up, and there were long minutes before the announcer could convey that Fitch, of America, was second, and that Butler, who ran second in this event to Rudd, the South African, at Antwerp, was third and Johnson, of Canada, fourth. Thrill followed thrill, for the flags went up, a big Union Jack in the centre, a little one to the left, and a little Stars and Stripes to the right, and again came that hush as all the spectators stood and the bands played. Then came crash upon crash of applause as Liddell walked across the grass and vanished down the stairs to the dressing room.

Liddell, in fact, was in a hurry to get back to his hotel room to prepare the address he was going to deliver the next day at a service for the athletes.

Back at the hostel in George Square, Edinburgh, George Graham-Cummings heard the news of Liddell's victory and world record in the 400 metres on his home-made crystal radio set. 'The announcer was so excited he could hardly speak! I myself was almost choking with emotion. Never have I experienced so much excitement over a radio broadcast as that one.'

Liddell's time in the 1924 Olympic 400 metres remained a European record until 1936, when Briton Godfrey Brown clocked 47.3 seconds in a semi-final of the 400 metres at the Berlin Olympics. His world record was not the fastest ever run for the distance, however. The American Ted Meredith recorded 47.4 seconds for the 440 yards in 1916. Curiously, his record did not count for the 400 metres, even though the former distance is two metres longer, a decision later reversed. But there were no sour grapes from Meredith, who watched the race from the stands. He had nothing but praise for Liddell's courageous run. 'Considering the condition under which he ran,' said Meredith referring to the extreme heat and the fact that Liddell was in the outside lane and had to set his own pace, 'it was nothing short of marvellous. Liddell,' he contended, 'was the greatest quarter-miler ever seen.'

Liddell's emphatic victory in the 400 metres had a far-reaching effect on the way the event was perceived from then on by athletes. Prior to the 1924 Olympics, the 400 metres and 440 yards were considered middle-distance events more akin to the 800 metres than the short sprints. Few sprinters of Liddell's class were prepared to take on the longer distance which required greater stamina. As former Scottish athlete John Keddie has astutely obser-ved, 'In this one race, Liddell almost single-handedly, implicitly (and unintentionally!) introduced a new con-cept of quarter-miling.' His unexpected victory in the 400 metres demonstrated that sprinters could compete effec-tively at the longer distance at the highest level.

The last word regarding his momentous victory lies with Liddell himself, and it was one that appears totally out of character. Captain Christison went back to the hotel after the 400 metres final to congratulate him. In reply, Liddell made it clear what he thought about nationalism. 'Nice of you to put the pipes up for me. I don't think it put an extra yard on me. Don't forget, I wasn't running for Scotland. The Olympics are not like that. We've had enough of struggles between nations. They are individual events to find out who is the best in his particular event. I ran for myself to prove that I was the best in my event.'

Strangely, Liddell made no mention of running for the glory of God as he had so often throughout his career. Could it be that he was angered by the accusations of betraying his country and being a traitor. Or was it a glimpse of Liddell the pacifist? Unlikely, for Liddell who, caught up in a wave of patriotism, volunteered for the Royal Air Force (RAF) at the ripe old age of 37 when he returned to Britain at the outbreak of the Second World War. Perhaps it was then just a manifestation of the competitive spirit which would not allow him to be beaten by a bus or, a decade-and-a-half later, to go for a casual jog with his missionary colleague in China.

5

THE LAURELS OF VICTORY

Eric Liddell arrived at Victoria Station in London with the rest of the British Olympic team to a tumultuous welcome. Simultaneously in Edinburgh, Scotland, two university dons – one a professor of Greek – were busy arranging a celebration of a different kind. Liddell was to graduate from Edinburgh University on the morning of 17 July and, to crown the Olympic hero, the professors had enlisted the assistance of the Keeper of the Royal Botanic Gardens, who supplied a sprig of oleaster (wild olive leaves) to form a laurel wreath. Meanwhile, to mark the occasion, the Professor of Greek composed a magnanimous eulogy in Ancient Greek.

The University's McEwan Hall, with its dome clad in gold leaf and frescoes, was a suitably illustrious setting for the graduation ceremony. There were a number of distinguished luminaries waiting to receive their honorary degrees that morning, including the historian G.M. Trevelyan and the Editor of *Punch* magazine, Sir Owen Seaman. *The Scotsman* newspaper, however, reported the next morning:

It was quite apparent that those present had been reserving themselves to greet the Olympic victor. As Mr Liddell stepped forward to receive his ordinary degree of Bachelor of Science, the vast audience rose and cheered him to the echo. The cheering continued for an appreciable time and there were several calls for silence before Sir Alfred Ewing (the Vice-Chancellor) could make himself heard.

George Graham-Cummings recalled the day Liddell received his degree. 'The Hall was packed to the rafters, but Eric simply sat in his place with everyone else in alphabetical order, just one of the boys as he always preferred to be. When his name was called, pandemonium broke out! The roar went on and on as he walked forward and then on and on as he stood before the Vice-Chancellor. Finally it died down and the Vice-Chancellor said, "Well Mr Liddell, you have shown no one can pass you but the examiner . . ." The rest was lost in thunder . . . Eric took it all with a good-natured, slightly embarrassed, but happy smile.'

Liddell was seized as soon as he left the Hall, thrust into a sedan chair, hoisted on to the students' shoulders and carried through the streets of Edinburgh like some Greek deity to St Giles Cathedral where the traditional post-graduation service was held.

As Liddell reached the steps of the ancient Cathedral, he felt compelled to deliver a short speech. Taking the inscription that crowned the gates of Pennsylvania University as his theme, he declared, 'In the dust of defeat as well as in the laurels of victory there is glory to be found if one has done his best.' Those who had done their best yet failed to win the laurels, asserted Liddell, deserved as much honour as those who received them.

At the graduation lunch, the eminent historian Sir Richard Lodge said in proposing a toast to 'Our Olympic hero' that he did not think he could remember so much of the 'ancient Greek spirit' about Edinburgh as he had that day. Liddell's reply was typically dry in its humour. He was a sprinter, he confided, because of a defect in his constitution. He was extremely short-winded and therefore would not detain them long. He blamed his unconventional style of running on his marauding antecedents who were wont to raiding England and were then forced to return more quickly than they came. That fleetness of foot appeared to have been inherited, and no one was concerned about running style when fleeing the pursuing English!

In a more serious vein, he concluded that man was composed of three parts – body, mind and soul – and it was only when all three were in harmony 'that they would get the best and truest graduates from the University'.

As the lunch came to a close, a group of university students drew up in a carriage. Liddell, still wearing his olive wreath, and the university principal were invited to step aboard and, accompanied by hundreds of students, the procession toured the city, encountering cheering crowds wherever they went.

The following evening, more adulation was heaped upon a slightly uncomfortable Liddell in the form of a litany of glowing tributes from those present. Liddell's reaction to the lavish encomiums was recorded by *The Scotsman*:

> The shouting and cheering suddenly ceased and he began to speak. The modesty and simplicity and directness of his words went straight to the heart. No adulation, no fame, no flattery can ever affect this youth with the clean-cut features, the level eyes and the soft voice.

He has got that great redeeming gift, the gift of humour
. . . He made us quickly realise that running was not to
be his career. He was training to be a missionary in
China and he was to devote all his spare time, until he
set forth for the East, in evangelistic work among the
young men in Scotland.

The *Student* said of Liddell:

Success in athletics sufficient to turn the head of any
ordinary man has left Liddell absolutely unspoilt and his
modesty is entirely genuine and unaffected. He has
taken his triumphs in his stride, as it were, and has never
made any sort of fuss. What he has thought it right to do,
that he has done, looking neither to the left nor to the
right and yielding not one jot or tittle of principle either
to court applause or to placate criticism.

Courteous and affable, he is utterly free from 'gush'.
Devoted to his principles, he is without a touch of
Pharisaism. The best that can be said of any student is
that he has left the fame of his university fairer than he
found it, and his Alma Mater is proud to recognise that
to no man does that praise more certainly belong than to
Eric Henry Liddell.

Eight days after his Olympic triumph, Liddell demonstrated that his victory in the 400 metres was no aberra-
tion. At Stamford Bridge in London, in a contest
between the British Empire and a strong United States
team, he ran the anchor (final) leg of the 4 × 400 relay. As
he was handed the baton, he was around seven metres
down on old rival, Olympic 400-metres silver medallist,
Horatio Fitch. Undaunted by the magnitude of the task
that lay before him, he set off in pursuit of Fitch, catch-
ing him in the back straight with a terrific burst of speed.

Fitch responded by holding Liddell round the final bend but could not match the latter's finishing speed in the home straight. Liddell opened up a gap of 3.5 metres and broke the tape in a sub-48-second time which could have been as low as 46 seconds.

In the following season, prior to his departure to China, he competed in meetings all over Scotland and made his farewell appearance at the Scottish AAA Championships in Glasgow in June 1925. An ecstatic crowd of 12,000 saw him in superb form equalling his own Scottish record of 10.0 seconds in the 100 yards and then achieving Championship bests in the 220 yards (22.2 seconds) and the 440 yards (49.2 seconds). The latter was the first occasion on which 50 seconds had been broken at the Championships and was to stand until 1957.

Liddell's last year in Scotland was one of feverish activity. Through the London Missionary Society he had been offered a provisional teaching post at the Anglo-Chinese College in Tianjin in northern China – provisional on the basis that he received his degree. Now that his position was confirmed, he decided to prepare himself for involvement in the religious activities of the College by enrolling on a theology course at the Scottish Congregational College in Edinburgh.

As well as studying divinity and continuing to compete in athletics, Liddell threw himself with great enthusiasm into the student evangelistic campaigns that became a phenomenon in the 1920s. He had already participated in a number of pre-Olympic evangelistic meetings organised by D.P. Thompson and the Glasgow Students' Evangelistic Union – of which he was now president of the Edinburgh branch – and it was Thompson who was in the vanguard of the so-called 'Manhood' campaigns.

It is difficult now to appreciate in our tired and cynical age the impact of these student Christian crusades.

Vibrant and energetic, the doctrine that the students preached was in marked contrast to the staid, stuffy conservatism of traditional religion. A Scottish newspaper wrote in September 1924:

> Several students from Glasgow University are in Ardrossan this week conducting an evangelistic campaign, and consequently we are hearing fresh voices, if not a new Gospel. Whether staid and respectable church-going folk are disposed to agree with all the methods of the students or not, we think that such campaigns are needed in these days . . .
>
> Their theme is familiar enough, but they have come with fresh enthusiasm to present it in their way and from their angle. They preach a strong, virile message, related to the problems of the day, which they believe to be essential to right the wrongs and transform the life of individuals and society.

The idea was to promote the concept of 'muscular' Christianity; that one did not have to be a wimp or a bore to be a Christian; that manly, sporting types could embrace the faith. And of course, blond, blue-eyed, Olympic champion Eric Liddell was the perfect example. 'Playing the game of life in a manly and Christian way,' was how the *Glasgow Herald* described it:

> Their leader, Eric Liddell, has struck that note in all his addresses. He stands for the Christian youth with a clean breeze about him and his lungs filled with the air that blows from the Judaean hills. There is not a tincture of conventional piety about any of them; they are interesting and winning. We wish them all the best kinds of success and a closing service that will crown their eight-day effort.

'I think it was just a very simple Christian message,' recalled Mrs Elsa Watson, who as a 14-year-old had established the Eric Liddell Club. 'There was no difficult theology to understand. All that he said, as far as I can remember, I could write on the back of a postcard. I understood what he was talking about. He talked about what might happen tomorrow, and what he was thinking today, and his honesty was just flashing out there the whole time.

'Looking back, I don't suppose Eric was a wonderful speaker. But he was sincere and so electric . . . I mean, he shone. It wasn't like just going to listen to a good speaker.'

'In preaching he never expounded elaborate theories,' said Annie Buchan, reflecting on their days working together on the North China Plain, 'but suggested the possibility of a "way of life", lived on a higher plane – to use his favourite expression – "a God-controlled life".'

One of the linchpins of the evangelistic crusades was an assault on the demon drink. Liddell took the lead, delivering what turned out to be a controversial speech in Glasgow on the evils of alcoholism. Today, his comments would be regarded as nothing less than common sense. He contended that alcohol reduced life expectancy, destroyed a man's character and self-respect and precipitated poverty and unemployment.

Nevertheless, some took exception to Liddell equating alcohol with evil, accusing him of extremism, including one who signed himself 'Moderate Drinker of 74 years'. 'I am one of those who greatly admire Mr Eric Liddell as an athlete and sportsman; but it is with great regret that I observe that he has allied himself with narrow-minded, fanatical teetotallers . . . One can have no admiration for the person who advocates compulsory teetotalism for everybody. Having joined the extreme sect of total abstainers, Mr Liddell adopts their intolerant language. Witness his speech at a "temperance rally" at Glasgow last week. He said, "Drink took away from character; drink took away from a man all that was honourable."

'These statements are not in accord with fact. Applied to "drink" per se they are untrue; applied to drinking in excess they are true. There are thousands upon thousands of old athletes in the country – runners, football players, cricketers, golfers and others – who have not been abstainers, but who are living today in good health and prosperity, useful citizens, admired and venerated by their fellow countrymen for their honourable characters.'

Elsa Watson, however, refuted any suggestion that Liddell was a killjoy who took pleasure in spoiling other people's enjoyment. 'Oh, Eric was never like that. I don't think he went in for tirades against anyone. I think this was one of the reasons why he was so effective, he put it in such a humble way. More of a matter of suggestion than anything else.'

Throughout the autumn and spring of 1924–5, D.P. Thompson and Liddell travelled all over Scotland and England speaking in theatres, music halls, churches, schools and colleges, a variety of auditoriums and even a public house on a Sunday morning. Not a natural orator, Liddell, nevertheless, became a more polished speaker as time went on.

'Eric has made great strides as a speaker,' observed Thompson. 'You could hardly know he was the same man as six months ago. We are getting on very, very happily together. I have never known a finer character in all my varied experience . . . There has never been a hitch or a shadow in our friendship, and it is due to him almost entirely. He is pure gold through and through.'

Thousands turned out to hear Liddell speak, gripped by his sermon illustrations culled from the chemistry laboratory, the rugby field and the running track, and large numbers, particularly young men and boys, gave their lives to Christ. Weekend after weekend and often on consecutive nights during the week, Liddell found time to preach in between his college classes and athletics training. 'No place was too small, no meeting-house too insignificant and no audience too unpromising in numbers or in quality for Eric Liddell,' reminisced Thompson. 'The more inconspicuous the service, the happier he was to render it, glad to be of any help to those who were carrying on his Master's work.'

At one renowned school in the North of England, Thompson and Liddell were ushered into the headmaster's study. The latter was absorbed in his work, until he noticed their presence and looked up suddenly. 'The "Head" looked long and hard and steadily at us both, and then, with confident step and welcoming smile, he marched forward to me with outstretched hand, saying, "Mr Liddell, I presume!" I assured him, with a mischievous wink at Eric, that he had made a mistake this time, but he was not so easily convinced. Back to his desk he marched and took up his stand again behind it. Adjusting his glasses, once more he gazed intently at my friend. "Well," he said. "You may be Mr Liddell, but you certainly don't look an athlete!" Under my breath, I am afraid I whispered, "What a man for a head-master!"'

According to D.P. Thompson, the most remarkable evangelistic campaign of the series conducted in the mid-1920s occurred at the London Central YMCA. Not only was smoking allowed, but a jazz band was playing while students, including Liddell, went from table to table, chatting casually to those assembled.

'Certain conditions were attached to the conduct of that meeting. The men were to sit at their ease in sofas and armchairs; they were to be free to smoke and ask questions; there were to be no hymns; and there was to be no

Scripture reading – just a brief word of prayer at the start and no appeal for outward evidence of decision at the close. Carter would introduce us in a sentence each night; Eric would speak first and then I would follow straight on. It looked, we felt at the time, an almost impossible proposition from the point of view of the evangelist.'

But what Thompson and Liddell preached made a deep impression on those who listened and within five minutes every cigarette and pipe had been extinguished. At the meeting the next evening . . . 'I [Thompson] ventured to invite those who felt like it to meet us in the chapel at the close – just to think quietly about all that we had been talking of together, and to ask ourselves in God's presence what it was going to mean to each of us. More than thirty came, and that night Eric and I were busy in separate rooms until nearly midnight, dealing with men anxious about their lives.'

By Wednesday evening the attention of those in the meeting hall was riveted on Thompson and Liddell as they preached. 'Not a match was struck – not a cigarette lit. Not a man lounged back in his seat or removed his gaze from the table behind which we stood – there was no platform. At the beginning of the hour, I said that we were going to finish with an after-meeting in the chapel. More than eighty men came that night – young business fellows, university students, professional men beginning to make their way in the City.

'It was, with one possible exception, the most wonderful after-meeting I have known. We knelt in silence for the best part of ten minutes; then I tried to make clear just what full committal to Christ must mean. Then Frank Carter, who had been with us through it all – thinking, praying, planning, encouraging – stepped forward to the door and stood with his back to it. He knew these men well. He wanted them to know just what this step was going to mean to them and the YMCA in London . . . In the next room they would find a table, several sheets of foolscap, pens and ink. Would those who really meant business and were prepared to respond to any demand that might be made upon them for service, go in there and put down their names and addresses? Forty-three men did so, and I believe some very effective work, much of it quite unspectacular, came out of that hour of decision and dedication. It certainly gave us both a new concept of the range and variety there must be in "the technique of evangelism." '

The last 'Manhood' campaign that Thompson and Liddell conducted together, in Edinburgh, a few weeks before the latter left for China, did not get off to a very auspicious start. At the opening meeting on a Monday at one of the free churches in the city, there was a capacity crowd of 1,100. By Friday, attendance was down to 500 and Thompson was being criticised for hiring Edinburgh's largest auditorium for the Sunday meeting.

On Sunday evening, a queue 45 metres long stood waiting to enter the auditorium. By the time the meeting commenced at 8 o'clock, an overflow venue had been arranged at a church further down the road and yet still hundreds had to be turned away. The reason: Eric Liddell was speaking. 'It was striking evidence,' marvelled Thompson of the astonishing turnout, 'of the immense hold Eric Liddell had on the Edinburgh public – and a great sight to see the huge gallery of the Usher Hall packed with students of many nationalities. The fruits of that fortnight's work were many.'

As the time for Liddell's departure for China approached, valedictory meetings – including two church services on his last Sunday – were held on his behalf and attracted vast numbers of admirers. The next day (Monday), dense crowds gathered again to see Liddell conveyed from the Scottish Congregational College, where he had been in residence, to the railway station via a carriage adorned with ribbons and streamers and drawn by a group of students. Just before boarding the train, Liddell was urged to give a parting message. 'I'm going abroad to endeavour,' he cried, 'to do my part in trying to unify the countries of the world under Christ.' And he expressed the hope that those left behind would support this crusade, adding, 'Let our motto be, "Christ for the world, for the world needs Christ."'

As the train pulled slowly out of the station with Liddell shaking the multitude of hands thrust up to his carriage window by those who wanted a last touch of the Olympic hero, the milling thousands, cheering wildly and full of emotion, began to sing hymns. 'It was such a send off as no missionary going abroad has ever had in Edinburgh,' wrote a friend of the Liddell family. 'I was glad to be there.'

Not long after he left for China, there appeared in one of the Glasgow newspapers a humourous cartoon portraying Liddell in clerical collar and running gear on the track, leaving his rival competitors trailing a long way behind. Beneath it was a rhyming quatrain:

> For China now another race he runs
> As sure and straight as those Olympic ones,
> And if the ending's not so simply known –
> We'll judge he'll make it, since his speed's his own.

A new race did indeed await Eric Liddell, no less daunting than the one he faced on that hot afternoon in Paris, a challenge that would consume the rest of his life.

6

RETURN TO THE FAR EAST

The China that Eric Liddell left in 1907 and returned to in July 1925 had undergone momentous changes in the intervening years. The corrupt and ailing Qing Dynasty had crumbled in the wake of a series of uprisings instigated by the gentry and mutinies by government troops in 1911. Sun Yat-sen became president of a provisional republican government and when elections were held in 1913, the Nationalist Party won a majority in the National Assembly in China's first and only free elections.

In a vain attempt to unify the country, Sun Yat-sen was forced to resign as president in favour of Yuan Shih k'ai, a former Manchu viceroy, who quickly seized absolute power and dissolved the parliament in January 1914. The short-lived democracy followed by Yuan's dictatorship did little to alleviate the suffering of the masses or bring peace. Lacking an effective army, Yuan was unable to control the warlords, who traversed the country with their private armies fighting each other for supremacy and raining death and destruction upon a defenceless populace.

If there was one issue, however, which united Chinese of all classes, it was an all-consuming hatred of the West.

The latter half of the nineteenth century and early twentieth century was a period of unmitigated disaster and ignominy for the Celestial Kingdom. The ease in which Britain defeated China in the First Opium War of 1839–42 exposed the latter's economic and military weakness, which was quickly exploited by the European powers.

Forced into accepting a series of humiliating economic and territorial concessions, China was systematically carved up into spheres of influence and barely survived complete dismemberment. To rub salt into the wounds, the century closed with a disastrous defeat at the hands of another Asian power, Japan, in the Sino-Japanese War of 1894–5, in which China lost Taiwan and its centuries-old influence over the Korean peninsular was severely weakened.

At the outbreak of the First World War (1914–18), China proclaimed itself non-belligerent, but then joined the Allies and declared war on Germany and Austria–Hungary in August 1917 in the hope of receiving some respect for its sovereignty and territorial integrity after the war. The Treaty of Versailles (which China refused to sign), however, was a bitter blow to China's attempts at freeing itself from imperialist subjugation. The Japanese were allowed to retain the territory they had seized from Germany and their concessions in Manchuria. Britain and France, flushed with victory, were in no mood to surrender their pre-war concessions and economic privileges to a weak Asiatic power.

The Washington Conference of 1922 addressed some of China's grievances, notably the return of Qingdao to Chinese rule, but the nation's sovereignty was still compromised by the unequal treaty system. The deep sense of betrayal and humiliation felt by the Chinese at their country's shabby treatment by the Allies fuelled an explosion of nationalistic fervour – dubbed the 'Fourth of May Movement' – which triggered a succession of nationwide strikes. Between 1919 and 1921, there were more than 170 strikes involving 250,000 workers. In 1922, Chinese strikers in Hong Kong closed factories and tied up ships, paralysing the economy. A few weeks before Liddell left Scotland, the Shanghai Incident of 30 May 1925 ignited a further wave of anti-foreign sentiment that spread rapidly across the country.

On 14 May 1925, employees at a Japanese-owned cotton mill in Shanghai went on strike in protest at the dismissal of fellow workers. The protest was joined by students, who demonstrated on 30 May and were fired on by the colonial police, suffering heavy casualties. Following the 'May 30th Massacre', the nascent but growing Communist Party extolled Shanghai workers, merchants and students to strike under the slogan 'Oppose Imperialism'. The strikes and boycotts spread quickly to other centres populated with foreigners, including Tianjin, where the Anglo-Chinese College was a conspicuous target.

At the same time, anti-Christian sentiment, which had remained relatively dormant since the Boxer Rising in 1900, was, in the wake of an explosion of nationalism, manifesting itself again. 'The missionary,' remarked an observer, 'was one of the tribulations imposed by Western Imperialism. Like railways, extra-territorial rights and foreign control of the Customs, he became a symbol of Chinese humiliation; and those who adopted his faith began to be seen as traitors to the Chinese cause.'

Eric Liddell, sitting in his carriage as the train trundled slowly eastwards via the Trans-Siberian Railway, must have pondered long and deeply upon his father's *Reports for 1924 and 1925*. Wrote James Liddell in 1924:

The past year has seen another Civil War, and the change of President, as well as a whole series of changes in the personnel of provincial positions, both civil and military. At the same time, the country has been brought to a sad condition with regard to railway communication and commerce. It is rather feared that parties are being rearranged in order each to test the strength of the other in the spring. The feeling all round is one of suspense, not knowing what will happen next.

To those who look on, it seems that no party is strong enough to command obedience, and really govern the country. The government of any one party is flouted by some other, although that other may have sworn loyalty to the one in power. It is not surprising that during part of this year Church work has been so difficult . . .

This year we have had the triple evils of war, flood and famine. Any one of these is bad enough, but all three together has made for suffering that is very hard to realise. Ruin has overtaken great numbers of families, and it will never be known how many lives have been lost, and may still be lost, through these visitations.

By the following year, the situation in China had deteriorated considerably as James Liddell's *Report for 1925* testified:

Last year I said there was a 'stirring of the waters'. This year one should say that 'the waters are boiling'. Words fail to convey to one not conversant with ways Chinese, the conditions that exist at present, and the variety of influences at work make a forecast impossible. The grievances of China have been magnified beyond all recognition. So complex is the situation, so varied are the views expressed, so opposite the conclusions reached, so many the solutions suggested, that one staggers beneath the crushing load. A nation is in travail, seeking to produce that which will meet all its aspirations. Whether it will do so or not is another question.

Before Liddell entered the fray, however, he would spend six pleasant weeks at the seaside resort of Beidaihe, preparing himself for the start of the college term in September. A week after Liddell arrived, Rob and his wife arrived and the whole family were reunited for the first time for several years.

In September 1925, Liddell arrived in Tianjin, Shandong Province, a Treaty Port second only to Shanghai in importance. Wrote one of Liddell's future colleagues: 'It is a city of glaring contrasts, where exists side by side, mansion and hovel, flaunting wealth and desperate poverty, modern enlightenment and age-long superstition, three universities and scores of schools, together with widespread illiteracy, and finally, extremes of climate with an annual range of over 100 °F.'

The inequality was most conspicuous in the division between the spacious foreign concessions and the densely crowded and insanitary Chinese city. Surprisingly, it was in the French Concession that the London Missionary Society was based and it was here in what was known as the 'London Mission' that overseas workers were housed.

When Liddell joined the family they were comfortably ensconced in No. 6 Mission, a spacious, four-storey house with a tennis court. 'The home was the centre for us all from which we each went our various ways,' recalled his sister Jenny. 'Father with his Church in town and country districts, often having to be away for days at a time; visiting, teaching, preaching, meeting with the Chinese pastors, etc, etc; Ernest going to school, but always at home at meal times, home lessons, etc; I, a pupil teacher in the kindergarten of the British grammar school; mother looking after the home, and doing a certain amount of work among the women, going out with the Bible women visiting homes, helping to entertain visitors – her name stood for generous hospitality, and a "home from home" for many a young missionary. And ever and always she was trying to improve her Chinese language, pouring over the characters in the Bible and hymn book.

'I can remember Eric getting all sorts of and sizes of test tubes for the college laboratory, and going over and checking their stock. He was expected to teach Pure Science, but was given various other classes in English as well, much to his own amusement. He began to prepare his lectures and to plan his term's work, once he had got settled in.'

Among those waiting to greet Liddell at Beidaihe Station had been a group of his future colleagues who had had the embarrassing duty of explaining to him that the College was currently being boycotted by its pupils, who, either of their own volition or under intimidation, were demonstrating their solidarity with the 'May 30th Movement'. By September, however, the intensity of the strikes and demonstrations was beginning to diminish and when the autumn term commenced that month, 150 pupils registered – much to the relief of the College staff – with the rest trickling back over the coming weeks.

A splendid, grey, towered building, the Tientsin Anglo-Chinese College, the 'Eton of China', offered an academic training steeped in Christian values to 500 boys, many of whom were destined for top positions in politics and the civil service. Founded in 1902 by the dynamic and academically brilliant missionary Dr Samuel Lavington Hart, the school, with a staff of five British and twenty-five

Chinese masters, had adopted an intimate tutorial system, with classes usually remaining with the same masters throughout the duration of their stay.

The College had the distinction of being the first to pioneer the playing of sports in north China. When Lavington Hart established the school at the beginning of the century, it was considered undignified for students to discard their long blue gowns and exert themselves on the sports field.

'There was little idea of what we understand by the word sportsmanship,' recalled Lavington Hart with amusement. 'Football was played and races were run in long gowns; a few drops of rain were enough to stop a game; if one side had no chance of winning, it wouldn't begin; if one player had his shins kicked, whether by accident or otherwise, he would leave the field in high dudgeon, carrying with him, by protest, the whole team; disputes with the referee were of frequent occurrence.'

Sports were considered essential for fostering Christian ideals of courage and fair play. 'The fundamental aim of this College,' asserted A.P. Cullen, one of Liddell's senior colleagues, 'is the upbuilding of Christian character and the formation of habits and mind and will and thought that will stand these lads in good stead when they face life's wider conflict. How is this to be done? Look at the playing fields. In no department of life has a greater change come over Chinese students here. In no realm of moral quality have the students, of Mission schools especially, made greater progress than in the realm of true sportsmanship.'

With Eric Liddell now on the staff, the College dominated school sports in north China, particularly the athletics team, which won just about every event it competed in under Liddell's guidance.

Liddell threw himself into College life with typical energy and enthusiasm, but as a teacher, at least in his own eyes, he proved to be a disappointment. He was clearly aware of this fact when he wrote dejectedly, 'I never seemed to get a grip of the class.' Perhaps the role was too formal for him. Liddell had an affinity with children and often displayed a distaste of disciplining them as a businessman in Weifang (formerly Weihsien) internment camp observed twenty years later.

Or could it be that he was being too hard on himself? Certainly many of his former pupils would not agree with his harsh self-analysis. One of them is former Hong Kong legislator Cheng Hon-kwan. He learned physics from Liddell, whom he remembered as a 'popular teacher, very enthusiastic but also very self-effacing'.

Bill Toop was another of his students, and it was Liddell's sense of fun that he remembered most. 'He taught chemistry and he used to insist we use all our senses. He said, "When you see something, you must grasp it entirely, the smells, the weight, the dimensions." On this occasion, he had a bowl of fluid on a bench and he asked us to dip into it and tell him what it was like. So we told him it was a liquid and described the colour and smell and he said, "Did you taste it?" Whereupon he put his finger in and tasted it. We did the same – and it was absolutely foul! It turned out that he had put in one finger and licked another. He was a great one for pulling your leg.

'If you had to use one word to describe Eric it would be integrity,' continued Toop. 'You only had to look at him and you knew any dealings you had with him would be absolutely on the level; you were dealing with a man.'

Whatever Liddell's shortcomings as a teacher – real or imaginary – he more than made up for them by his involvement in the religious life of the College. A worship service was held each morning, and the teachers, in rotation, would speak on a passage of Scripture. With his gift of commanding attention, Liddell soon became one of the most popular speakers.

Of more spiritual value were the weekly Bible Circles held in each class and conducted by the class tutor outside school hours. Informal as ever, Liddell held his at his home. 'In my own class,' wrote Liddell, 'only three out of the thirty-eight come from Christian homes, but seventeen come to the Bible Class. I have been taking the Life and Times of Jesus with them. They each have a daily Bible reading card, with instruction as to how to use it with advantage. By this I hope to get them into the habit of (1) Quiet morning prayer; (2) Expectation that the Bible has a message for them which can be applied to their own lives day by day.

'One boy came to me asking for baptism so I put him the direct question as to why he wanted it. He said that one night when he was at prayer he had a deep sense of sin, and that while he prayed the whole burden of it was taken away. The other day, two of my class came along asking for baptism. They had not attended my Bible Class as they lived too far away, but the message that had come to them day by day at morning prayers in our hall had led them to the decision. Although they come from non-Christian homes yet their parents are quite willing for them to take this step.'

This was what Eric Liddell had travelled thousands of miles and sacrificed a glittering career on the running track for – to impart to his charges the joy and conviction of his faith.

'He was a completely dedicated disciple of Jesus Christ,' wrote Tianjin flatmate David McGavin, 'and a man who could not rest short of nothing but the introduction of those brought under his influence to the

Saviour and Master who had come to mean so much to him.'

'His Bible Classes, out of school hours, were very well attended,' recalled another friend. 'I remember the joy with which he would tell us of boys who had committed their lives to Christ. He was never too busy to see or talk with any Chinese student who called and how they loved him. I think 90 per cent of his students joined the Bible Class.'

The task of gently guiding his pupils into the embrace of Christianity was not without its struggles and disappointments, but bore fruit throughout his years at the Anglo-Chinese College. 'The class has not been an easy one,' reflected Liddell, 'and it has driven me to a deeper life of prayer myself. There was one boy who was specially irritating, so I put him down for special prayer. After several months, I came to know one of his big problems, and should have pressed my advantage, especially as I had passed through a similar difficulty, but I'm afraid I missed the chance. This year he has been much better, and for a time joined the Bible Class, but there's a long way to go with him yet.'

As head of athletics at the College, Liddell took the opportunity to revive his own running career, and he was soon to prove to the world that he had lost none of the speed and determination that had earned him the epithet, 'the greatest quarter-miler in the world'.

7

AN INCORRUPTIBLE CROWN

In an athletics booklet entitled *Get to Your Marks*, compiled by Ross and Norris McWhirter (published in 1951), there appeared a curious entry for 1929 in the world-ranking list for the 400 metres: 'Liddell, E. – 49.0 secs: date not known – somewhere in China.'

Few people in Britain were aware that Liddell took up running again in China, let alone the fact that he was recording world-class times. To the aficionados who did, it was a surprise that he was not invited to join the British team for the 1928 Olympics in Amsterdam. That he was not called upon to represent his country again was probably because the British AAA assumed that once he left for China he was no longer available for selection.

There is little doubt that Liddell could have made a major impact at the Games, a fact forcefully underlined a few weeks after the Olympics when he clocked 21.8 for the 200 metres and 47.8 for the 400 metres – equalling the winning times at Amsterdam. And that was without any training!

A *Peking and Tientsin Times* correspondent commented in October 1928:

A man who can improve on 47.8 for the 400 is a marvel. Knowing Liddell as I do, it can be taken for granted that his comment (that he could improve his times with training) was not a boast, but merely an honest statement of fact. He is a non-smoker and does not drink, but it may be easily understood that however good his normal condition, special training would have given him that extra edge so necessary for Olympic standard. My own opinion is that Liddell is still the best quarter-miler in the world.

Far from exuding the air of an Olympic champion, Liddell cut quite a shabby figure in his long, baggy navy blue shorts. Quiet and unpretentious, he let his running do the talking. 'He made no fuss over his start as they did,' observed a spectator. 'Just stood and waited for the gun, and then trotted gently down the course – the only point being that his gentle trot took him past and far beyond all the other competitors, who were straining every nerve, and brought him to the winning post with the others trailing yards behind.'

'He gave some marvellous performances, particularly in running for the Anglo-Chinese College in the International Sports,' reminisced a British soldier stationed in Tianjin. 'He will never be forgotten by the soldiers who were out there. He had an outstanding personality, being so utterly unaffected by his successes on the track.'

More proof was provided of Liddell's form and fitness when he competed in a meeting grandiloquently entitled 'The South Manchurian Railway Celebration of the Coronation of the Emperor of Japan' in Darien in northern China in 1928. Against opposition from the Japanese and French Olympic teams fresh from Amsterdam, Liddell easily won the 200 and 400 metres.

Years later when he was an evangelist visiting war-torn villages on a Japanese-occupied North China Plain, he was often recognised by Japanese troops who remembered the meeting and this helped to ease the tension between the two.

It was following this meeting that Liddell ran his most extraordinary 'race' ever, the legendary 'boat race', featured in the British *Victor* comic. The last event of the meeting was the 400 metres, just thirty minutes before he was scheduled to catch a boat back to the Anglo-Chinese College. With a taxi standing by, he calculated that he could just get to the quayside in time. Having duly won the 400 metres, his pace barely slackened as he sprinted for the taxi, when 'God Save the King' suddenly pierced the air, requiring him to come to an immediate halt and stand to attention only agonising metres from the taxi. But that was not the end of his ordeal. 'Then, of course, I was about to leg it for the taxi – but what do you think happened then? Well, you'd hardly believe it, but the fellow who came second to me was a Frenchman, so of course, they had to start the 'Marseillaise', and there I was, tied like a post again! The taxi made it in great time. I took a healthy hop, step and leap, and was on the edge of the wharf before it stopped. The boat was steadily moving out – too far to jump. But a bit of a tidal wave threw it back a little. Then I flung my bags on to the wharf and jumped. I tried to remember in the very act how a gazelle jumps. I felt like one, and I made it; just made it.'

A newspaper correspondent watching from the taxi claimed Liddell leapt four-and-a-half metres that day. Modest as ever, Liddell queried the distance, but whoever was correct it was a staggering leap which only added credence to his sobriquet, 'Flying Scot'.

A year later in Tianjin, he competed against the great German runner, Dr Otto Peltzer, holder of the 500 metres, half-mile and 1500 metres world records. Liddell won the 400 metres, Peltzer the 800 metres. In the pavilion after the track meeting had finished, Peltzer said to him in broken English:

'You represent Britain at the next Olympics?'

'No,' Liddell replied, 'I'm too old.'

'How old?'

'28.'

'Too old?' Peltzer replied, roaring with laughter. 'I am 32, and I will represent Germany at the next Olympics.'

And he did. Later he told Liddell, 'You train for the 800 metres and you are the greatest man in the world at that distance.' However, after 1930 Liddell never competed again in public in a major athletic meeting.

Did he ever regret missing the 1928 Olympics and the chance of winning at least another gold medal? Did he lament trading fame and glory for a life of obscurity and hardship? He gave clear and unequivocal answers to these questions when interviewed in Canada at the end of his first furlough in 1932.

'Are you glad you gave your life to missionary work? Don't you miss the limelight, the rush, the frenzy, the cheers, the rich red wine of victory?' probed the interviewer in rather florid prose.

'Oh well, of course it's natural for a chap to think over all that sometimes,' replied Liddell. 'But I'm glad I'm at the work I'm engaged in now. A fellow's life counts for far more for this than the other. Not a corruptible crown, but an incorruptible one, you know.'

According to his wife Florence, he would have been content making a living playing billiards. 'I think at one time he would have been quite happy to live by his wits in some kind of sport. But that was before he met D.P. Thompson.'

In 1929, Liddell's father's period of missionary service came to an end, and with it a halcyon sojourn when the family were united for the last time. The Reverend James Liddell's departure for Scotland necessitated the surrendering of the family home, and Liddell moved into a flat belonging to the Anglo-Chinese College with some close friends. Two of those, Dr George Dorling and David McGavin (who moved in some time later) regarded the years they shared a flat with Liddell as among the richest of their lives. 'He was the life and soul of a holiday or expedition,' reminisced Dorling. 'How well I remember him at Pei-Tai-Ho [Beidaihe] singing "Under the Spreading Chestnut Tree".'

The flat they shared was spacious with a dining room and sitting room. Meals were provided by a Chinese cook. Breakfast was at 7.30 a.m., afternoon tea at 4 p.m. and dinner was usually English cuisine. Despite busy, demanding schedules, there was always time for conversation and recreation. Liddell had a bit of a reputation for being 'very hot stuff at billiards'. Unfortunately McGavin, who had just arrived, was unaware of this and was astounded by his potting ability and complete mastery of the cue. 'I can see where your misspent youth was spent,' remarked McGavin after being given a thrashing by Liddell.

Said McGavin, 'Eric was not only one of Nature's gentlemen, he was a perfect Christian gentlemen, and therein lies the secret of all he was and did. His life was centred in Christ and everything was done as to the Lord. It is said that really to know a person one must live in the same house with him. This was my privilege when Eric and his two colleagues invited me to share their flat in Tianjin, and I found that, at home, as elsewhere, Eric's life glorified God.'

He recalled an incident that was typical of Liddell's utter selflessness. 'While on holiday together at Pei-Tai-Ho, during the summer of 1931, we called, one morning, at the home of some friends. After greeting us, the lady of the house said, "You're just in time for coffee. Do sit down." Soon the cups, saucers and biscuits were laid on the table, and, while our hostess went off for the coffee, a fly settled on the topmost biscuit. Since all of us had to be careful what we ate, I remarked to Eric, "Don't touch that biscuit, a fly has been on it," but this was the biscuit that Eric was careful to take. His action was not intended as a rebuke to me – that would never occur to him – but to make certain that no one else should suffer discomfort as a result of eating the biscuit defiled by the fly . . . Eric was the most Christ-like man I ever knew and there are many who, like me, thank God for every remembrance of him.'

The bachelor life, however, was coming to an end for Eric Liddell. In 1929, at the age of 27, he met a 17-year-old school girl, fell madly in love, and much to the amazement of his friends, asked for her hand in marriage.

8

MARRIAGE AND FATHERHOOD

When Liddell announced casually in July 1930 that he was engaged to be married, most of his friends were stunned. 'I didn't even know he was courting,' said one, ship's engineer Bob Knight.

Such was Liddell's subtlety that even the subject of his attention, 17-year-old Florence Mackenzie, the daughter of Canadian missionaries, was blissfully unaware of the depth of his feelings. They had met at the Union Church Sunday school in Tianjin, where she played the piano and Liddell was superintendent, and she had been in his brother Ernest's class at school.

'It was in the summer of 1929 that Eric and Flo did their courting,' recalled his sister Jenny. And one can imagine Liddell pursuing the young girl he had decided to marry. Shy, bashful, the winsome smile; ever one for playing practical jokes, yet gentle and chivalrous – the perfect gentleman. A British soldier who was a friend of the Liddells and the Mackenzies wrote, 'It was with great delight that I first learned that she was to become the wife of such a charming personality as I knew Eric to be.'

'I was terribly naive,' Florence recalled with amusement. 'Eric had become such a part of the family that I just didn't notice anything. Of course I was desperately in love with him, but I couldn't get over the fact he wanted to marry me. It never dawned on me that he would ever propose. So when he did I was quite stunned. I said, "Are you sure you really mean that?" And he said, "Yes." There were several girls of his age and I thought, "They're going to kill me!"'

'It was in the summer of 1926 on our return from our second furlough,' wrote his future mother-in-law. 'One evening when my husband and I entered the vestibule of Union Church to attend the weekly prayer meeting, Mr and Mrs James Liddell were there and introduced us to Eric, whom we had all heard about. I remember he was very unassuming and so gentle in his manner.

'Words fail to describe a personality like Eric's, with his natural goodness and great single-mindedness. He was completely filled with the Spirit of Christ, bringing peace and gladness wherever he went. I remember one evening he dropped into our home, saying he had been called by a businessman who was seriously thinking of ending his life. After a talk with Eric, this man had changed his mind. Eric was at home amongst rich and poor, business people or missionaries and with all nationalities.'

It would be four more years before the couple married. Florence returned to Canada to study nursing, while Liddell went back to Scotland via Toronto on his first furlough in the summer of 1931.

Seven years may have passed since he won the Olympic 400 metres, and he may have been, according to one observer, 'a little yellower and balder', but he was still regarded as a national hero and was in great demand as a speaker by both the religious and sporting worlds.

The year that followed his return was a whirlwind of activity as Liddell spoke on subjects ranging from his old favourite, the evils of alcoholism, to Chinese nationalism at packed halls and rallies throughout Britain. Commented one who attended a Liddell meeting, with a sense of awe: 'For twenty minutes, he held 300 football fans spellbound with his honest but simple words, delivered in a quiet voice with a kindly persuasive smile. At the finish, he got a standing ovation.'

Particularly courageous was his decision to speak at a series of meetings in Belfast, Northern Ireland, on nationalism in China. 'In a city such as Tientsin,' explained Liddell, 'there are colleges in what are termed the Concessions – areas taken over by foreign powers. Chinese public opinion, strengthened by a growing national feeling that other nations had taken from her what should be hers, has been asking that these Concessions should be given back.

'I don't want to go into the political aspect of the question, not being a politician myself. But just glancing at the matter, I feel it would be extremely difficult to give this land back immediately; but our policy – and the people in Tientsin are trying to do it – is gradually to hand it over. I think that this method will not only cause less complications between nation and nation, but is the most Christ-like way in which it can be done.'

Few people ever saw Liddell run again after 1925 and he did not compete on the track during his first furlough, although D.P. Thompson believed that he contemplated running in Scotland. One of the very rare appearances he did make occurred when he returned to his Alma Mater, Eltham College, to present prizes on sports day. Missionaries' son and Eltham old boy Edward Patterson still vividly remembered the occasion sixty years later: 'He was asked to take part and at first declined. But everyone wanted to see him run, so finally, reluctantly, he came to the starting line for the 220 yards – in his ordinary walking shoes and with his jacket over his arm. He won by a mile!'

Somehow, among his speaking engagements and public appearances, Liddell found time to study for the ministry, and on 22 June 1932 he was ordained as a minister of the Scottish Congregational Church. Thus it was that he returned to China that summer as the Reverend Eric Liddell. But before he left, there occurred an incident at the church of a minister friend of D.P. Thompson which again demonstrated the depth of his compassion for humanity.

'When he left after a happy visit in January 1932, Eric signed our visitors' album and then added a group of Chinese characters with the translation: "Keep smiling",' wrote the minister.

'Eric,' I said, 'there's a member of my congregation who will be thrilled to see this. She'll hardly be able to read it. Her scalp and one eye were torn out in an accident at her work five years ago. She suffered two years of agony having skin-grafts and a succession of operations which miraculously pulled her through and restored her to a measure of health. Periodically, intense headaches prostrate her; she is nearly deaf; once a month, all the eye lashes on her remaining eye have to be pulled out, for, as a result of the skin-graft, they grow in upon the eyeball. She can just see with that eye, but she will be thrilled to look at these characters, and to know that they represent in Chinese the motto she adds at the end of every letter she writes: "Keep smiling." She'll feel they are a message you've left specially for her.

'"But," said Eric, "I'd like to meet her. Would she mind?" Would she mind! She talks about it to this day, for Eric did visit her, busy though he was that week, and chatted with her for an hour in her little room. And after his visit, Bella as her custom was, wrote him a long letter of thanks, in which in her simple way, she told of some of the occasions on which God had used her and her affliction to help others.

'It was some weeks after that I heard the sequel. Eric received her letter just as he was leaving his parents' house to catch a train to London. He read it through twice, then put it in his pocket and settled down into a corner. There was only one other passenger in the compartment, a young man. His dejected attitude, his bearing and manner of utter depression attracted Eric's attention. He got into conversation with the young fellow and soon the whole story came out.

'It was a common enough story of adversity and failure, aggravated in the young fellow's case by some special circumstances of personal defeat, so that he had lost all belief and hope and was seriously contemplating suicide.

'Afterwards, Eric confessed that for a few minutes he did not know what to say or do that might help his companion. What he did was to pull the letter from his pocket and say, "Read that." And he went on to speak of the woman who wrote the letter, her life of grinding hardship, her accident and the responsibilities she was still carrying for other people; above all, the faith in which she was enabled to face all these things and still keep smiling.

'Before that journey ended, a new journey had begun for that young man, and Bella, when she heard of it, was proud and happy to think that a little letter, slowly traced by a barely-seen pencil in her shaky hand, had been used by God and a great Christian soul to save yet another from darkness to light.'

Liddell returned to China via Toronto again to visit Florence and her family. He also had the opportunity to chat with and impart some advice to the British Olympic team, who had stopped over in Toronto en route to the Los Angeles Olympics, for some extra training.

Arriving in Tianjin in September, and with his marriage not for another eighteen months while Florence prepared for her nursing exams, he busied himself decorating and furnishing the house they were going to live in, and attended to his duties at the Anglo-Chinese College, which had become even more onerous. In addition to preparing for lessons, marking exam papers, holding Bible studies and being sports coach, he was now secretary of the College, which he took over from A.P. Cullen, chairman of the Games Committee and in charge of Religious Activities. In whatever spare time he had he was also preaching regularly at the Union Church, leading a Bible study for men and continuing to learn Chinese.

'If next month is to be an easier one as regards teaching and meetings, this one has been crowded enough,' wrote Liddell to his mother. 'On Thursday, I was leading the Hai Ta Tao Church Prayer Meeting; on Friday the Ku Lou Men's Bible Class. On Saturday, I was to lead the Student Christian Fellowship, which is really a bit better than it was, but what a long way I have to go yet . . .

'There isn't much time for reading: it always seems to be giving out rather than taking in; a bad thing, I know, but perhaps safer than erring on the other side. I'm still on the subject of the Holy Spirit at Ku Lou Hsi. How I long to see us all get a real great baptism of him.'

In the autumn of 1933, Liddell's father, who had been such an influence and source of inspiration to him, died suddenly. Eric was finishing breakfast when he received the news and sat in stunned silence recalling the immense amount of love, sacrifice and service contributed by his father during his years on the mission field. He said later that he felt his father was very close to him as he preached at the Union Church on the Sunday on which he died. To a bereaved mother in Scotland, the devoted son wrote a stream of letters offering solace and comfort:

'When this letter reaches you near the end of February the first flowers of spring should be starting up. Surely by then the snowdrops should be out, and a little later will come the crocuses and daffodils. Jenny's garden will soon begin to bloom again. You must go out there, Mother, and stay with her, especially at that time of year. I am glad that I have recently had a furlough and been with you, for now I can picture it all so clearly and seem to know what you are doing.'

Having passed her nursing exams, Florence set sail for China and arrived in Tianjin at the beginning of March 1934. The ship was delayed, however, and Liddell, nervous and excited, could hardly bear the waiting. 'We arrived back in time for tea at 4.30. How difficult it is when you are thinking all the time about them coming to be sociable to the others. Then we got news that the boat was in the river about 6 p.m., and we could see the lights, so we hurried off. It was slow in coming in – just desperately slow – and it had two shots before it got there. We couldn't see the people on board and they couldn't see us, but we called out. Florence was just the same as ever.

'We had missed the last train up that night so I slept in the lounge after we had just talked and talked. Florence and I got up early next morning and caught the 5.30 train up to Tientsin, getting there at 6.30. We breakfasted together and decided on the colour scheme for the rooms in the house and got through a lot before going to meet the boat with the rest of the family, due in at 10.30.'

Eric and Florence were married on 27 March 1934 at the Union Church, and after a reception at Florence's parents' home they left for their honeymoon in the Western Hills outside Beijing. Arriving back in Tianjin two weeks later, his schedule was no less demanding than it had been in his bachelor days.

Japan had annexed Manchuria in 1931, forming the puppet state of Manchukuo, and was now encroaching on China's northern provinces, making conflict ever more likely. Wrote Liddell, 'By orders from the Government one of our classes has to take military drill and although I hate war, and feel the attitude of Christian people to it is going to be one of the challenges in the future, yet it has smartened up some of the lads quite a bit.

'I've been glad that for the first time I've been able to gather some of the teachers each morning for prayer and thought before the day's work started. It has helped us all in Christian growth and also in our attitudes to others and the smoother running of things in general. One of the staff who hitherto did no Christian work has started a Bible Class in a lower form. I hope this will grow and that we will steadily find the Will of God a clearer thing in our lives and also obedience to it a greater delight and joy.'

Two daughters – Patricia and Heather – arrived in quick succession, and Liddell turned out to be a typical proud father, as his letters home testify, expounding in detail how his first daughter was walking by herself and trotting all over the place. 'Patricia loves sitting on a small seat I have on the bar of my bike, and we go round the compound or out into the street. Heather is as good as gold. She sleeps soundly through the night and hardly disturbs us from the 10 p.m. feeding till the 6 a.m. one. The idea of not having a 2 a.m. feed from birth is a good one. We've found it the best thing with both of ours. Last week, Heather put on 6 ounces . . .'

Dry as Liddell's humour might have been, he could never resist a practical joke. Just before Heather was born, he thought he would play one on Florence. 'She was supposed to be a Christmas baby,' recalled Florence. 'If she was a girl, I wanted to call her Carol. Eric wanted Heather. Finally, he said, "Let's draw lots." He prepared the papers and I drew and the paper had "Heather" on it. That was all right with me. But afterwards, Eric showed me that he had written "Heather" on each piece of paper. I remember throwing a cushion at him. But I felt that if he wanted the name Heather that badly, he could have it.'

Little did they realise that this blissfully happy period of family life between 1934 and 1937, of idyllic summers spent at the seaside village of Beidaihe, would be the longest they would ever spend together. Soon they would be separated for long periods, and finally, forever physically.

In June 1935, Liddell was asked by the LMS District Council whether he would consider going to Xiaochang, a village on the North China Plain – where his brother Rob was already working as a missionary doctor – to work as an evangelist. Not only was there a desperate shortage of missionaries in the countryside, but the Anglo-Chinese College was considered to be straining available resources by retaining an overly large contingent of LMS staff. Liddell declined the request on the basis that his Chinese was too poor and he didn't feel 'a definite enough call to give up his educational work'.

The matter would arise again, however. In 1936, the District Council decided that Liddell should be released from his College duties for four months to experience 'country work' first hand. By the following year, with the Anglo-Chinese College under pressure to relinquish one of its foreign salaries, and after much prayer, Liddell decided to go, despite intense opposition from his colleagues. In fact, many chided him for being foolish for abandoning all he had accomplished at the College. 'It really hurt him,' said Florence. 'But he never let on. That was one place where I learned he could take criticism.'

'Perhaps we shouldn't have been so critical,' reflected Stanley Thompson, Head of Maths at the College. 'But he was doing a good job at the College and we missed him.'

Liddell's resolve remained firm, but it was a deeply distressing decision to have to make. The LMS decided that with the outbreak of the Sino-Japanese War in July 1937, Xiaochang was too dangerous for Florence and the children to accompany him, so he was faced with the prospect of being separated from his family for months on end after only a few years of marriage. 'It was a big step involving many changes and it took him a long time to be sure he was doing the right thing,' said Florence. 'However, after much prayerful consideration of all the points involved, he felt God was calling him to the country, and I think it was quite obvious he did the right thing. He loved the work, his health improved and I think he blossomed out in a new way.'

This view was reiterated by Liddell himself. Despite the separation, he never expressed any doubts about his decision. 'It is good for me that in a year of unprecedented hardship and suffering for the people,' wrote Liddell in the autumn of 1938, 'I should be sent away from the city and that the journey down here should have given me such an opportunity of seeing some of the hardest hit places between here and Tientsin.' Annie Buchan once asked him if he ever regretted leaving the comparative comfort and security of the College and

Tianjin. 'Without hesitation he said: "Never! I have never had so much joy and freedom in my work as here."'

9

WHAT COULD GOD
HAVE DONE?

In December 1937, Liddell and his brother Rob – who was rejoining the mission hospital staff – reached Xiaochang after a ten-day journey, mostly by riverboat. A small village on the North China Plain, it was the centre of the London Missionary Society's evangelistic outreaches in an area ravaged by war, drought, famine and disease.

Surrounded by a mud wall, the LMS compound consisted of a hospital, school, living quarters and a church which could act as a refuge for hundreds of women and children during the worst of the fighting. Perched above the front gate was a sign declaring in Chinese characters 'Chinese and Foreigners, All One Home', put up after the compound had been rebuilt following its destruction during the Boxer Rebellion.

Shortly before Liddell arrived, the Japanese had launched a full-scale attack on China on the pretext of a minor military incident at the Marco Polo Bridge fifteen kilometres outside Beijing. Aided by the inability of the Kuomintang and Communists to settle their differences and fight the common enemy, the Japanese quickly occupied the major cities and lines of communication in northern and eastern China, but were never able to fully subdue resistance in the countryside. Flanked by the two main railway lines controlled by the Japanese, hardly a day passed without the LMS missionaries and staff in Xiaochang hearing the clatter of machine-guns and the explosion of artillery shells.

Liddell was under no illusions about what awaited him. Letters from Rob, who had arrived in Xiaochang in 1928, and Annie Buchan, matron of the hospital, had prepared him for the horrors in store. She had written of how she witnessed Japanese soldiers plundering the poverty-stricken villagers:

'Now we are seeing them at work, kicking open doors, pushing their swords through them, hearing the cries of the terrified people inside . . . of fellow missionaries shot by bandits; of being forced to watch a group of bound prisoners paraded through a village street, followed by an executioner with a long carved knife dripping with blood. Every so often the column stopped and he lopped off a few more heads, tossing them into a basket hung above a pavement.'

This was the savage milieu in which Liddell became an itinerant evangelist, covering a vast area either on foot or bicycle; visiting churches, advising Chinese pastors, helping the hard-pressed peasants in any way he could. Such was the Communists' antipathy towards Christians – Roman Catholics, for instance, were shot without trial – that Liddell had to pose as one of the hospital staff with the title of 'hospital accountant' and wore a Red Cross armband when out in the countryside.

Many people in the district still remembered his parents and he received a warm welcome wherever he went. 'He was often used as a buffer if there was a quarrel,' recalled Annie Buchan, '"Li Mu Shi [Li stood for Liddell; Mu Shi means pastor in Mandarin Chinese] will settle it." If there was a difficult problem to solve, "Ask Li Mu Shi what he thinks."'

His colleagues praised his sympathy and patience in dealing with what they considered to be a superstitious and backward people, his cheerfulness under all circumstances and his willingness to undertake the humblest task without complaint. 'Looking back on that time,' reflected a colleague, 'one can realise how much we owed to his unconquerable spirit. Our tempers and nerves were strained and frayed by constant alarms and excursions, and by unexpected responsibilities and decisions, but it is possible to realise more fully now how much his faith and confidence meant to us all.'

Liddell himself has left some vivid images of life on the North China Plain during this turbulent and strife-torn period in Chinese history, observed as he cycled round the district.

'At Ming Shih Chuang, I met evangelist Wang Feng Chou, who was to go with me. His home is in Nan Kung, so he knew the way. We start with a short prayer for guidance each day. The people in the village were busy spinning thread and as the making of native cloth this year brings in so much, the people are all busy at it. The crops in Nan Kung have been largely a failure – only three to four tenths of the usual – and so the making of the cloth is helping people to find a living.

'As the sun was setting, we reached Wang Feng Chou's village and he found me a place to stay. I stayed in the home of the father of one of the Siaochang School boys. It was a very large family of some twenty odd. Last year, cholera carried away four of the family within a very short space of time. Each day, I went out to nearby places and had meetings in the mornings and the afternoons, leaving about 4 p.m., so as to be back before the sun set. The whole of this area is riddled with Eighth Route Army [Communist] troops. Schools are opened and all below forty-five are forced to go to them.

'It was wonderful to feel oneself one with the people. I remember one night, being in a very poor home for supper. The small light was so poor that its rays only lit up nearby objects. There was the faint outline of a spinning loom. All day long they work at it right into the dark hours of the night; click, click, click, it goes all the while I sat with a bowl of chiao tyus! The man of the house was with me. In the dim light, the wife could be seen every now and then attending to the fire and preparing food. The girl was on the K'ang; what a girl too. She used to come to the evening meetings and I can see those great longing eyes looking up into my face, so eager, so expectant, just like the child in *The Light of the World*.

'As the meal drew to a close, two young men from next door appeared with their bowl of gruel. They squatted on the floor and started chatting about English customs and ways of eating. They would laugh and then they asked me to speak English. Soon we would be singing and then the same piece in Chinese. I'd teach them the Chinese and while they sang in Chinese, I'd sing in English and we'd all laugh. And so, for the time being, we forgot the sorrows of the present in the laughter of fellowship.

'But in the country places far from the cities, there is little amusement. Life is very quiet, very dull and there is hardly any fun. Most of the year, people have to work long hours and there is little else to do, even for children, than to work. It is no wonder then that they look forward to the travelling theatre that comes to most villages once a year and stays five days.

'Then what a change takes place. How the bairns crowd and watch the putting up of the great stage and the dressing rooms for the actors. When the opening day comes, the people put on their best garments. The women and girls are dressed in very brilliant clothes and have their faces powdered and their hair adorned.

'The folk gather from far and near. Some on foot, others – think of the fun! – on barrows, many on very large wagons carrying as many as twenty people and a few arrive in their own private carts. Perhaps 800 to 1,000 persons gather and crowd in front of the wide platform. Most squat on the ground, others sit on their carts. It is all in the open air.

'For five days straight on the plays continue, from 11 on the forenoon till about 10 at night. They are entertained for two hours and then rest for two, so that the audience may eat and sleep. And what fun they are! Shouts of laughter all the time and music most of the time. For five days, all the dullness of the past months seems forgotten in the laughter and joy.'

Children, whether his own or other people's, always had a special place in Liddell's heart, and the abuse and neglect suffered by many Chinese peasant children touched him deeply. Girls, then as now, were often unwanted in a society that placed a premium on sons, and many were abandoned or killed at birth.

Liddell reported in an LMS magazine:

> When you go to the Far East, to countries where Jesus is scarcely known, you find next to nothing is done to help the weak and distressed. This is especially true of the children and of girls in particular.
>
> I think of a little girl who was badly treated, for she was not wanted. Her Chinese people left her in the open air in the cold in such a way that her feet were badly

frostbitten – so badly that when she was found by a lady missionary, her feet had to be taken off. But with great care she got well and strong and wooden feet were made for her. Years afterwards, I found that she had married and that her children taught how love can help and heal.

And yet I think of another little girl who had been sold to a family, where she was made a slave. She was beaten and ill-treated so badly that she became very ill. Someone found her and took her to a Christian Hospital, where all the terrible treatment she had received was seen in the marked and dreadfully bruised body. At the Hospital, everything was done that skill could do and after months of careful nursing and medical treatment, she was made well and strong. She too experienced how love found her, helped her, healed her and brought her new life. Jesus means us to pass on to others his love in deeds of kind thought, remembering that what is done for one of his little ones is done for him.

Dr Kenneth McAll, the mission hospital's surgeon, often accompanied Liddell on his evangelistic trips to the country.

'We were shot at many times and put into prison, but the Japanese knew Eric's name, so we always got away with it,' recollected McAll. 'Perhaps they remembered his appearance at the Far Eastern Games in Port Arthur.'

It was not only Liddell's fame as an athlete that helped to ease the tension between the missionaries and Japanese soldiers. His natural friendliness and humanity extricated them from many a menacing situation.

'He handled the Japanese with the same cheerful charm,' recalled a colleague, 'and would reply to savage or shouted queries with a beaming smile and perfect good nature. The Japanese were then indulging in a campaign of petty persecution to try and get rid of the

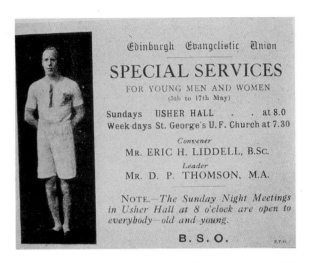

Liddell first spoke at an evangelistic rally in 1923 at Armadale, West Lothian.

Eric became British Champion at the English AAA Championships winning the furlong and the 100 yards.

Eric prepared for the Olympics throughout winter
1923 with his trainer, Tom McKerchar.

Eric at his graduation being carried on friends' shoulders. (Photo courtesy of University of Edinburgh.)

The Anglo-Chinese Christian College where Eric taught pure science for 12 years.

Eric ran Sunday services and midweek meetings in Tianjin. Here seen with a Bible study class.

Eric and Florence with their daughters, Patricia and Heather, in 1940.

Eric in Xiaochang, China.

'I press towards the mark for the prize of the high calling of God in Christ Jesus.'

Xiaochang missionaries, but against that smiling calm their efforts broke time and time again. He was asked to the military HQ to answer questions and he cycled off alone to the town, seven miles away. The gendarme tried threats, warnings and accusations in vain: Eric remained cheerful but quite firm.'

Wrote Liddell: 'Sometimes it has been easy passing the sentries and sometimes it has taken a long time. I think I have had nearly every type of experience. They have searched my shoes to see if I had secret letters hidden in them. On seeing my compass, they at once said, "May I have that please?" or something to that effect (in Japanese of course!). I told them it was of more value to me than to them.

'Once when I was in Sang Yuan waiting in the Inn, the Japanese military came in to inspect all luggage. As I opened mine, the man's eyes fell on the New Testament. In slow and broken English he said, "Bible – you Christian?", held out his hand and shook mine, then turned and went.'

Florence recalled that the mission was confronted with the problem of paying its staff when the Japanese introduced their own worthless currency. The helpers at the mission were still paid in Chinese currency, but anyone found in possession of the money was liable to be shot on the spot. Liddell's solution was to smuggle the money into Xiaochang by stuffing wads of bank notes into a hollowed-out French-style baguette.

'As soon as he got off the train and was asked for his passport, he whipped out his wallet and started showing the guards pictures of the children. Well, they responded with pictures of their own and it was smiles all round and slaps on the back as they sent him on his way – oblivious of the contraband money even though the loaf protruded conspicuously from the top of his haversack.'

In a country where law and order had broken down and extreme violence and death were commonplace, it was not surprising that some of the mission staff considered carrying a firearm for protection, including Kenneth McAll. That was until he told Liddell of his intention.

'I had had the thought of carrying my own pistol and was offered a very nice one which attracted me. Eric said, "Don't you dare touch that thing! Put it down! Don't even handle it!" I said, "Why not?" He replied: "Don't you realise that these people know what you're thinking. You will be shot long before you get to your pistol. If you're trusting in God and are absolutely peaceful and thinking about how you can help that person, they will know that. They'll put their pistols down. They won't shoot." And he was absolutely right, because one would relax with a rifle in your back or a pistol on your forehead and say, "Lord, what do you want me to do?" And the guerrilla or Japanese would put their weapon down and want to know who you are anyway because they had never encountered this sort of reaction before.'

In his book, *The Moon Looks Down* (Darley Anderson, 1987), McAll illustrates one of the many occasions when he and Liddell cycled across the fields and unmade roads in search of wounded, left to die after the numerous skirmishes between the Japanese forces and Communist guerrillas. Liddell was setting his usual cracking pace and McAll decided to stop, but the former was too far in front to hear. Suddenly, a hail of machine-gun bullets passed between the two bicycles. Miraculously, neither man was hit.

Divine intervention? Liddell would certainly have thought so – McAll's drawing of an angel hovering over his head reveals how he interpreted the incident. 'Those early morning "quiet times" were the key to everything,' explained McAll. 'We would sit for about an hour, listening as well as talking to God. There was complete silence, and often we were both smiling as if at a private joke. Eric always looked as though he was enjoying a private joke and he always thought very deeply before replying to a question.'

For all his tremendous respect and admiration for Liddell's commitment to living an uncompromising Christian life, McAll feels that there was a certain narrowness in his approach to life. 'He had a one-track mind. If he felt God was telling him to do something, then he would do it,' said McAll. 'He was always challenging me about spreading myself too thinly. He once said, "Please can you make up your mind what you want to be: are you a missionary, a surgeon, an evangelist or an artist? Find out what God wants you to do and just get on with it." I just thought to myself, "You haven't got any other talents, bad luck to you!"'

McAll remembered another example of Liddell's single-mindedness. 'I used to go for a jog occasionally and I once invited Eric to join me. He said, "When I run, I run to win. I will never jog, but I will go for a stroll." If anyone else had made that remark they would have appeared arrogant, but Eric said it with such a delightful smile.'

As the conflict between the Communist Eighth Route Army and the Japanese intensified, more and more villages were being wiped out and thousands slaughtered. 'A lot has been made of the 200,000 killed by the Japanese in Nanjing,' said McAll, 'but I would say that as many if not more were killed within the vicinity of Xiaochang while I was there. We would have to dig mass graves – we'd bury 250 in one evening. When the Japanese came to a village they would shoot all the men, rape all the women, eat all they could, take all the animals and we'd get all that was thrown away.

'They slaughtered thousands. I remember a man was accused of spying for the Japanese and was about to be executed by the Communists. One of the villagers stood up for him and told his captors that he was a good man who had fed the village in times of famine. This man was immediately dragged out of his house and executed as well. When it came to brutality, there wasn't much to choose between the Communists and Japanese.'

McAll remembers one of the mission's Chinese pastors being caught in the countryside by the Communists. Despite protesting his innocence, he was accused of being a spy and was ordered to dig a hole and get in it head first. He was to be buried alive with his feet sticking out as a warning to others. However, it was decided that he should be given a chance to prove that he was a mission-ary after all by reciting hymns. Fortunately, he was able to sing a number of hymns without making a mistake and was released. Hundreds were not so fortunate and suf-fered a gruesome fate at the hands of their captors.

The mission hospital was often overwhelmed with wounded as the war in the countryside intensified. Kenneth McAll was amazed at the peasants' equanimity and endurance as they waited patiently for treatment, often after walking many miles to the mission. 'The patients are wonderful. After a long journey of say four days by cart, and then to be told that nothing can be done [sic] – with little or no change of expression, they rise to start the journey home,' wrote McAll in May 1939. 'One day I had to amputate a T.B. woman's feet, the next day several wanted to leave and others extracted a promise from me that I would not remove their feet too.'

The missionaries themselves were often called upon to assist the medical staff by boiling surgical instruments and changing dressings. One of them, Alex Baxter, was appalled by the total indifference displayed by the local

Chinese leaders and their reluctance to provide any assistance.

'We begged for food for our refugees, but they would neither give us grain nor a stove to boil grain. Nothing showed more clearly the fundamental, even startling difference between the Christian outlook and the non-Christian. One would have expected them to share something of the heavy burden of the mission. They had seen us caring for hundreds of their own people. We had cared for hundreds and the mind cannot face the thought of what happened to the many hundreds more who could not come to us.'

The suffering that Eric Liddell witnessed as he travelled from one village to another affected him deeply. He wrote of a house he came across which had been destroyed by the Japanese:

'It was one of those pathetic scenes which must be so familiar now, but which never ceases to stir the emotions – a ruined home. Great long pieces of burnt timber – every bit of the home gutted by fire, except two rooms. Here, two widows and their two girls stayed. The Japanese came. The man was taken and because no ransom was forthcoming, he was shot and the two widows struggle on to face the world. I bowed in the courtyard and asked God's blessing upon them, but the words seemed almost to come back to me, "What could God have done?"'

Another incident, recalled by Annie Buchan, again reveals the anguish and helplessness felt by Liddell when a man was dragged out of his house for questioning and, when he refused to co-operate, was summarily shot. 'I had nothing to say,' remarked Liddell afterwards. 'I just stood there and then I said, "What could God have done?"'

'He had such sympathy,' reflected Buchan. 'Never a lot of talk, but you could see it on his face. Always on his face.' We constantly had casualties in a terrible condition, but there was one especially awful one at Huo Chu. Eric found a man just outside the village. The Japanese thought they had beheaded him – he was a stout man of 40 – but they hadn't. He had a very deep, wide slash round his neck. He had been lying there for five days like that before they found him.

'Eric was there. I remember his face. On those occasions, you just had nothing to say. But the emotion was there on his face.'

Liddell described the incident in a letter home in 1939:

'When journeying back from Tientsin to Xiaochang my colleagues and I heard of a wounded man, lying in a temple, twenty miles from our Mission Hospital. No carter would take the risk of taking wounded men, for fear of meeting Japanese troops on the way. However, one Chinese carter said he would go if I accompanied him. They have a wonderful confidence in us!!! It would be quite dangerous for him, but I think there was no danger so far as I was concerned.

'On Saturday, February 18th, the carter started on the journey, and some hours later I cycled after him. By evening the carter reached Huo Chu, 18 miles from Siaochang, where we had our Mission premises. I cycled on to Pei Lin Tyu, three miles further on, to see the Headman of the village and make arrangements for the wounded man to be removed. He lay in the temple about 100 yards outside the village. The temple is a filthy place open to the wind and dust. No one ever comes along to clean it.

'No home was open to the wounded man, for if the Japanese descended on them and found that a home had anything to do with the military, it would be destroyed at once, and the lives of those in it would be in danger.

'For five days the man had lain in the temple. A friend came there daily to feed him. He lay on a thin mattress on the ground. When we remember that the nights and days are cold and that every night the temperature would be at freezing point, if not well below it, we marvel that he was still alive. The Japanese (a tank and ten motor lorries) were at the next village a mile away.

'I told the wounded man we would be back early the next day, and then I returned to Huo Chu. That night, as I lay down, wrapped in my old sheepskin coat, my thoughts turned to the next day. Suppose I met the Japanese, what would I say? I felt for my Chinese New Testament, a book I constantly carried with me. It fell open at Luke 16. I read until I came to verse 10, and this seemed to me to bring me an answer. "He that is faithful in that which is least is faithful also in much: and he that is unjust in the least is unjust also in much." It was as if God had said to me, "Be honest and straight." I turned and went to sleep. We started early next morning. As we approached the first village, there was a man standing in the entrance to it, beckoning us in. We entered the village and as we passed through it the Japanese mechanised troops went round it. We fortunately missed each other.

'Many of the roads had been dug up, and were like enlarged trenches, and in clambering out our cart overturned.

'We reached Pei Lin Tyu early in the day and went to the temple. It was Chinese New Year's Day. People were in the temple burning incense. They were even burning it at the side of the wounded man. I asked the people to come out. I gave them a talk on fresh air being of more value to sick and wounded than air laden with incense smoke. Then I turned to those great words from Micah – "Wherewith shall I come before the LORD . . .? shall I come before him with burnt offerings . . . He hath shewed thee, O man, what is good; and what doth the LORD require of thee, but to do justly, and to love mercy, and to walk humbly with thy God?" [Mic. 6:6,8.]

'We laid the man out in the cart and left. On reaching Huo Chu, we heard of another wounded man whom we could pick up by going out of our way a short distance. We decided to go and see. When we reached Pang Chuang, we went to see the Headman. He and some others led us to one of the outhouses. Several men went in first to warn the wounded man that a foreigner was coming to see him, but that he need not be afraid. On entering, I could see, in dim light, a man reclining on a bed, dirty rags wrapped about his neck. He was one of six men who had been sur-rounded by the Japanese. They were told to kneel for exe-cution. Five knelt, but the sixth remained standing. When the officer came to him he drew his sword and slashed at him, making a gash from the back of his neck round to his mouth. He fell as dead. After the Japanese left, the vil-lagers came out and finding him alive, they had taken him to this outhouse where he had lain for several days.

'I told him my cart was only a small one, made for car-rying one person, but that if he was willing to sit in the shafts for eighteen miles (three hours), I would take him to Siaochang Hospital. I could not guarantee his safety; if we met the Japanese, he would have to take his chance.

'For the first few miles, a Japanese aeroplane was cir-cling round slightly south of us. It indicated that the Japanese troops were moving almost parallel to us a mile or so away. At 4 p.m., we reached the hospital. Two days later, the first man died, but the second lived. Treated first by Dr Graham and by Dr McAll, he soon recovered. His mind turned towards the Christian life and teaching and within a couple of months, he made the first steps in Christian living.'

Among all the misery, suffering and despair, there were always lighter moments to relieve the horrors of war.

Kenneth McAll remembers the night the Communists came over the mission wall, seized a patient from the hospital and shot him. The gunshot woke the nearby Japanese garrison, who showered the compound with mortar and machine-gun fire. 'I called Eric and told him of the problem and we both felt God was telling us that I should be the first one to inform the Japanese of what had happened. This, I thought, was the end of me.

'I went outside the hospital guardhouse and asked to see the garrison commander. I was taken to a little hut and inside there was a Japanese lying on a couch with his back to me who turned out to be a colonel. I tried explaining to him in Chinese what had happened in the night, but received no response. I then tried pidgin English, and when that didn't work, normal English. But still no reaction. Then suddenly, he shouted something in Japanese and the two guards ran out. He then rolled over and said, "Forget it buddy!" and I replied, "So you can speak English." "Yes, but don't you dare tell anyone. I was born in California, but I thought I would come and help my country. Now all I do is kill, kill, kill, and you do the opposite. I don't know what to do!"

'For the next week we met secretly to talk and drink tea. Later, I met him again quite by chance at Tianjin docks and discovered he'd got a transfer as Head of Customs.'

To escape the pressures of life in Xiaochang, the missionaries would occasionally spend a few days at Beidaihe, the coastal resort near Beijing where Liddell spent his summers as a child. During the summer, the sea was usually infested with poisonous man-o'-war jellyfish.

'To get rid of them,' recollects McAll, 'we would hit them very hard with a piece of wood. On one occasion, Eric was swimming underwater and one of the missionaries, Alex Baxter, mistook his bald head for a jelly fish and whacked it hard. Eric came straight out of the water and was livid. "Don't you ever do that again!" he shouted nursing a bruised head, to a startled Baxter, "You jolly well almost killed me!" That was the only time I ever saw Eric really angry.'

Liddell was absent from Florence and the children in Tianjin for months at a time, and then would suddenly appear without warning. Florence recalled with amusement what occurred on one of these occasions:

'The children had a habit in the morning of crawling into bed with me. One particular morning, Eric appeared in the night and the girls came as usual that morning. Heather, who was only about two years old, reared back when she saw this head beside me. "Who's this!" she said. "The cook!" Eric roared with laughter and said, "I knew we were friendly with the cook, but I didn't know it had come to this!" He didn't let me forget it for long time after.'

'The flag is still flying,' wrote Liddell, probably with more assurance than he felt, in July 1939, 'so don't get depressed. There is still plenty to thank God for.' However, the portents of war were gathering ominously in the Far East, as they were in Europe, as Liddell returned to Scotland for his second and final furlough.

10

STORM CLOUDS GATHER

By the time Liddell reached Scotland, Britain and Germany were at war and in a burst of patriotic fervour he volunteered for the Royal Air Force (RAF) with visions of becoming a fighter pilot. Considered too old at 37, he was offered a desk job instead. Typically, he turned it down flat with the comment, 'If you're only going to stick me behind a desk, then I've got more important work to do.'

It was to a different Britain that Liddell returned in 1939; a country preoccupied with war and fearful and uncertain of the future. And Liddell himself was a little older, and after two years in Xiaochang, a little more serious. The great rallies of his last furlough were not possible now, but to the audiences he was able to address, he tried to describe the complexities of the situation in China as accurately as he could in his characteristically simple way. A minister who heard him speak at a meeting in Manchester, England, wrote:

'It was just a simple portrait gallery, in words, of some of his Chinese friends and contacts. The audience, at first, was obviously puzzled by its extreme simplicity, for it was the first time most of them had heard this famous Eric Liddell, and they had come expecting rhetorical fireworks. But as the address proceeded, the audience became profoundly attentive. Those Chinese he described so vividly were in the room.

'This simplicity of his was, in truth, that rare gift of the childlike spirit of which the Kingdom consists, and before the address was ended, the audience was aware of it.'

In March 1940, Liddell was joined by Florence and the girls, and after completing his speaking engagements, he and the family returned to China via a ten-day stopover in Nova Scotia.

If Liddell's journey to Britain had been uneventful, the voyage back to China was fraught with danger. Britain was struggling to protect its merchant shipping against attacks from German U-boats which were sinking ships indiscriminately. In fact, it was a miracle that they ever saw the shores of China again. Off the coast of Ireland, their ship, part of a convoy of fifty, was hit by a torpedo. Wrote Liddell of the incident:

'It was 8.30 when the children were asleep. Whether it was a "dud", and only the cap exploded, or whether it had expended its energy, having been fired from too great a distance, or had exploded right below us, we are not sure. I would say that we were actually hit, and only the cap exploded, judging from the feel in our cabin. No alarm was given for us to go to the boats, but the signal for all boats to zigzag was given by ours.

'The next night we lost one of our ships at the back of the convoy. The sea was choppy – a very difficult one to spot submarines in. The escort left us that day. This was the hardest of all days. About 10 a.m., a small boat about a quarter of a mile from us was torpedoed, blew up and sank in two minutes; they must have hit the engine boiler. We were on deck ready for the boats, and everyone zigzagged. About noon, the "all-clear" went and we returned to dinner. We had just started, and were halfway through the first course, when the alarm went again. Another boat torpedoed. It didn't sink. We heard later that it was able to get along. Whether it turned back or tried to carry on, I don't know.

'We were still in convoy, but not escorted now. By teatime they decided it was too dangerous going on in convoy, so we broke it and each put on full steam ahead . . . It was a tense time right up to the next morning. At 6 p.m., word came through by wireless that the ships which had been sailing next to us, about 200 yards off for the last two days, had been torpedoed. Ten minutes later, another; and at nine o'clock at night we heard that a submarine had risen to the surface and was being engaged by one of the convoy in a running fight.

'The ship was running at full speed, far above its average. All night people slept in their clothes, with lifebelts ready. The next day the tension eased; we were going out of range of the ordinary submarines; only an ocean-going one could come so far, and caused numbers to be seasick again. Since then it has been calmer. No excitement; we have had enough for one trip.'

When Liddell returned to Xiaochang at the end of October 1940 the situation at the mission was even more precarious than when he left. The village was now garrisoned and surrounded by a high wall and it was clear that the mission's days were numbered.

'As I look out of my bedroom window, in the east house, the south village looks like one of the outposts of the Empire,' wrote Liddell grimly. 'The last few days we have watched rather depressed and dejected men going out on forced labour, to prepare a motor road to pass to the east of Xiaochang.

'Ruthlessly land is requisitioned without any compensation, ancient burial places and graves are disregarded as

the Japs gradually force their way further in and drive
their roots deeper. It is the people who suffer all along. It
makes you think of the old Roman press-gangs, and
brings with it the ever-increasing hatred and rebellious
spirit that these things should be.'

Liddell described in one of his letters home a wedding
ceremony he attended in one of the villages in his area,
conducted with the thud of heavy artillery close by.
After the service he and the other guests were invited to
a traditional Chinese wedding banquet.

After the bowing was over and the benediction pro-
nounced, we turned and went to where the bridal dinner was prepared. And so, in the midst of all the fears
and alarms, the world goes on as if all were calm and
quiet. The heavier guns could be heard that evening
only a mile away, as they fired in the direction of the
people who were cutting up the road. But in Huo Chu
we just met together for a service of prayer, praise and
thanks, thinking about our contribution to a better
world; and the bridal pair spent their first night with the
sound of gunfire in their ears, but love and joy in their
hearts.

'I stayed on over Sunday, taking the service and chatting with the people. I should have returned that day,
but the cart I was expecting did not arrive till nightfall.
It had been delayed by the 8th Army, who were stopping
the moving of all carts. On our return journey today
there was little of incident except at one point. The
enemy must have taken us for the 8th Army and fired
two shots. We just got off our bikes and stayed still till
they realised their mistake, and then we went on.

'My work will be going round the various churches. I
now go out to the south-west to a part I never visited
before. When I am out it is giving, giving, giving, all the
time, and trying to get to know the people, and trying to

leave them a message of encouragement and peace in a time when there is no external peace at all.'

Japanese soldiers who had once kept their distance were now entering missionaries' homes, drunk and brandishing their swords menacingly. One day, Annie Buchan rushed into the hospital's operating theatre and found the doctor she was urgently seeking pinned against a wall, a soldier beating him with a baton.

'I want this doctor!' the diminutive Buchan cried, and the soldier stood back in sheer astonishment. But it was evident that the officers were no longer bothering to control their men.

Finally in the spring of 1941, the missionaries were ordered to evacuate the mission by the Japanese. A few weeks later, they heard that Xiaochang had been razed to the ground.

With internment or worse becoming more of a reality by the day, and with Florence pregnant with their third child, Liddell decided that his family had to leave for the safety of Canada.

'It was a very difficult decision,' recalled Florence. 'I didn't want to leave at all. But we were sure Japan was going to come into the Second World War. Eric could have come with us, but he didn't feel he should. He was worried that if they took us hostage, he wouldn't be able to trust himself. I never felt his work came first. It wasn't like that at all. He just felt others were staying and he ought to as well.'

'He knew the Japanese were stepping up the war and that internment was almost certain,' remembers Stanley Thompson. 'But he felt that if he went away and left his work and his people in Xiaochang then it would be running away, and he couldn't do that. So he had the dilemma of seeing his family go and not knowing really what was going to happen.'

The day she said goodbye to Liddell in May 1941 was still indelibly etched in Florence's memory just before she died in 1984:

'Finally, the day came for sailing and we got on this beautiful big ship. Eric was able to come on board with us. Then the whistle blew for visitors to leave. We were down in the cabin at the time, so Eric put Tricia on his knee and said, "Now Tricia, I want you to look after Mummy and help her with Heather and the new baby. You just take care of Mummy." She was five years old and she said, "Yes Daddy, I'll look after Mummy until you come back,"' reminisced Florence, barely holding back the tears.

'I was very upset when Eric left, but it never crossed my mind for a minute that I wouldn't see him again. Even right at the end, it never crossed my mind that anything could happen to Eric. I don't know how I could have been so naive.'

In September, Liddell received a telegram from Florence informing him of the birth of his third child Maureen – the daughter he was destined never to see.

Soon after his family's departure, he moved into a flat in Tianjin with his former Eltham College schoolmaster and Anglo-Chinese College colleague, A.P. Cullen. With no official duties to attend to, Liddell kept himself busy by working on his *Manual of Christian Discipleship*, which he hoped would eventually be translated into Chinese as a spiritual guide for Chinese pastors.

In December 1941, in the wake of the Japanese attack on Pearl Harbour, the members of the London Missionary Society were ordered to leave their homes in the French Concession. Liddell and six others were offered accommodation by members of the English Methodist Mission in the British Concession, and remained there until his internment in March 1943.

The missionaries were allowed freedom of movement, although they were not permitted to venture beyond the perimeter of the concession and had to wear armbands indicating their nationality. Assemblies of more than ten people, in or outdoors, were also prohibited, which effectively precluded church services. To circumvent the ban, Liddell had the idea of organising a number of missionaries to write a sermon for each Sunday. Their wives would then invite ten people to tea on Sunday afternoons. Sufficient copies of that Sunday's sermon would be produced for each tea party to have a home-based service.

Liddell had gone to live with the Reverend D. Howard-Smith and his family, and like his previous flatmates George Dorling and David McGavin, Howard-Smith considered the year Liddell spent with them as one of the most memorable of his life.

'Eric came to live with us, and for a year we had the privilege of his sharing our home,' recorded Smith. 'I never saw Eric angry. I never heard him say a cross or unkind word. He just "went about doing good", and he did it so unobtrusively, so self-effacingly and so naturally that one just took it for granted that Eric was just like that, because day by day he kept an early morning tryst with the Lord.

'The remarkable thing about Eric was the way in which he was never too busy to accommodate himself to the wishes of others and the way he could accept trivial things and duties. The boys wanted him to play cricket with them – then Eric was ready. My girls wanted him to teach them tennis – so out he went into the hot sun, with the temperature above 100 °F in the shade. He was needed for a four at bridge – so he joined in. He was interested in collecting Chinese stamps and when my girls wanted to collect them too, he spent hours preparing albums for them, with places marked for all the issues. He spent hours answering their questions with infinite patience and the same careful patience manifested itself when he was teaching a class in the Sunday school, or listening to the tale of woe poured out by some simple peasant from the country.

'When my wife was finding it difficult to get sufficient bread for the hungry family of six adults and two children, often finding the shops all sold out when she went to her shopping, Eric quietly volunteered to go each morning to the bakery at 5 a.m., and he went. My wife remembers a terrible dust storm such as we got sometimes in North China, when the dust comes into the house through closed doors and windows to cover everything. She went to bed resolved to get up at 6 the next morning and sweep through the house from top to bottom. She went down at 6, and found Eric, with dustpan, brooms and dusters, just finishing. He had quietly got up at 4.30, and without a sound to waken the rest of us, had done a thorough job. That was typical of Eric.'

In his letters to Florence, Liddell described how he made his days as productive as possible. As well as working on his discipleship manual and preparing for church meetings, he spent many hours in quiet meditation and study on such subjects as the work of the Holy Spirit, divine guidance and the Sermon on the Mount. He also devoted considerable time to compiling a series of daily Bible readings with notes for the whole year, a project he completed during his internment. 'If it never comes to anything,' wrote Liddell of the project, 'it will have been useful for my own thinking. And to me will always be a companion booklet to the *Daily Prayers* which I got out [this was published in 1942]. It would be easy to let this time go by with nothing done; nothing really constructive, and so have the days frittered away.'

To get out of the flat, Liddell would go for long walks with Cullen, exploring the Concession, or go out to dinner or tea with friends.

'He loved the good things in life as much as any of us,' recalled Cullen. 'How often, during the last phase in Tientsin, did he and I "celebrate" one of the many birthdays of our respective families by a modest dinner at the Europa Cafe (where you got perhaps the best value for your money!), or, if we couldn't run to that, a tea at the Cosy Club. But all his happiness – the happiness that shone so radiantly in his face – all his happiness had its basis in his serene faith in God, his love for God, and his appreciation of God's gifts.'

In August 1942, the possibility of evacuation presented itself again to Liddell, and though he was willing to stay, he put his name down on the list, writing to Florence about the possibility of setting up a 'Home Mission' in Canada. But it was not to be. The call for evacuation never came and Liddell, along with all the other foreigners in Tianjin, found himself in a rough, third-class train carriage bound for the Japanese internment camp where he was to spend his last and finest hour.

11

THE FINAL VICTORY

The bombing of Pearl Harbour by the Japanese on 7 December 1941, and the subsequent entry of the United States into the Second World War, sealed the fate of the remaining foreigners in the Japanese-controlled areas of China. It was only a matter of time before they would be rounded-up and interned, or even imprisoned.

Thus it was that on 12 March 1943, Eric Liddell and his colleagues in Tianjin received instructions – along with hundreds of other 'enemy nationals' – to report to the Civil Assembly Centre (a euphemism for internment camp) in the city of Weifang (formerly Weihsien), situated in the centre of Shandong Province, northern China.

Liddell was appointed captain of the missionary contingent of the British party, who were ordered to send their belongings ahead to the camp: each person was allotted three trunks and a bed and bedding. On 30 March, the foreigners, struggling with their hand luggage, were marched to Tianjin Station through streets lined with Chinese as a final act of humiliation – the white man's domination of the Far East had come to an ignominious end. A new imperialism had risen in the East to take on the mantle held for so long by the West.

After an exhausting sixteen-hour journey, they reached the camp, which was located two miles from Weifang in a ruined American Presbyterian mission. The compound, only 200 yards (183 metres) at its widest point and 150 yards (137 metres) long, contained a school, a church, dormitories, three kitchens and a bakery. Although the buildings were intact, the interiors had been wrecked by the Japanese in a fit of anti-westernism. Beds, radiators, pipes and furniture were ripped out and smashed and lay strewn in the streets.

As the internees straggled into the camp, its entrance crowned by a sign announcing the former mission's Chinese name, 'The Courtyard of the Happy Way' – and no doubt the irony was not lost on those who passed beneath it – the most depressing sight that met their weary eyes was the camp's toilets, which stunned even the most hardened among them. Langdon Gilkey, until then a young teacher at an Anglo-American University near Beijing, recalled the stench of the overflowing toilet bowls and, with some amusement, the shock of Westerners confronted with their fellow man's bodily waste.

'Life in Weihsien was a grim battle for survival,' remembered missionary Meredith Helsby. David Michell, who was 9 when he entered the camp, recalls the stench and 'the squalor of the open cesspools, rats, flies and disease in the kitchen–dining room where they were eating. On hot summer nights it hung low over the camp in sultry, pungent clouds.'

The 1,800 internees were a disparate group drawn from numerous nationalities and all walks of life: British, Americans, Italians, Belgians, Dutch, Indians, Palestinians, White Russians, even two Cuban families from a touring *jai alai* team. Whatever their previous employment, they had to quickly acquire new skills and develop the art of survival: executives unused to manual work had to learn how to bake bread and stoke fires, while prim, pampered society ladies, who had barely stepped foot into a kitchen before, became practised in scrubbing floors and washing dishes.

It was not long before life in the camp settled down to a drab routine: up at 7 a.m. to attend to chores and assigned work duties; roll call (which became twice daily after two internees escaped); queuing for the toilets and meals that failed to quell the constant, gnawing hunger. David Michell recalled the stultifying monotony of a typical camp menu. Breakfast: two slices of bread (often hard and flat if the yeast supply was low) and millet or sorghum porridge with sugar on very rare occasions; dinner or lunch – hash or stew, which included mushy eggplant, popularly known as S.O.S. ('Same Old Stew'), and occasionally dessert; and supper – usually soup, which was often a watered-down version of S.O.S.

Oswald Dallas, a resident of Beijing before he was interned, was a baker in Weifang and often had to use peanut shells to make bread when flour was scarce. 'It wasn't too bad when it was hot, but once it had cooled it was like rock.' A canteen was eventually opened by the Japanese and occasionally the internees could supplement their diet by purchasing items such as peanuts, eggs, honey and fruit when in season.

Mary Taylor Previte, whose great-grandfather James Hudson Taylor established the China Inland Mission, was 9 when she entered the camp. 'In the early days of the war, we lived on *gao hang* (Chinese sorghum), the roughest broom corn, or *lu dou* (green beans) cooked into hot cereal for breakfast, and all the bread we wanted.

'Only the stout-hearted could work in the butchery with the maggot-ridden carcasses. Plagues of flies laid eggs on the meat faster than the team could wipe them off. When the most revolting looking liver – horribly dark, with a hard, cream-coloured edge – arrived with the day's food supplies, the cooks called in our school doctor for a second opinion. Was it fit to eat? Probably an old mule he guessed. So we ate it.'

In an environment of stifling and interminable drudgery, it was not surprising that tensions grew, tempers became frayed and arguments broke out over what would be considered trivial in normal life. 'If you wanted to see the worst in people,' recalled an internee, 'you stood and watched the food line, where griping and surliness were a way of life. Hungry prisoners were likely to pounce on the food servers, who were constantly being accused of dishing out more or less than the prescribed half-dipper of soup. Shrieking women in the dish-washing queue hurled greasy dishwater at each other.'

Weifang was a microcosm of society: it had a hospital, laboratory, school and church. It also had prostitutes, alcoholics, drug addicts, scroungers and thieves, who stole extra food from the kitchen, and roving bands of bored adolescents. Lacking parental supervision, teenagers roamed the confines of the camp at night and there were even rumours of sex orgies in the basement of one of the camp's buildings. Jeannie Cotterill recalled the frustration that many of the young people felt about being cooped-up in the camp and missing out on life.

'One particular girl, who was extremely clever, said, "We'll never be able to get on with our education! We'll never get boyfriends!"'

'There was always this extra aggro,' recalled Cotterill. 'People's nerves were on stretch, thinking about what was happening at home. The only news the Japanese gave us was that, yet again, they had sunk the entire British fleet or that London had been bombed to smithereens for the fifth time. It was obvious rubbish, but we had no firm news of any truth and I think this was what really got people down.'

'One or two of the commandants were particularly intrusive,' remembered her husband Joe Cotterill, who was also in the camp (they married while interned). 'One chief of police was particularly cruel. He got the name of "King Kong", mainly because of his physical build. But there didn't appear to be any deliberate policy of intrusion. There was a curfew every night. We weren't allowed outside the dormitories between 10 p.m. and, depending on the time of year, 6 or 7 in the morning. All the toilet facilities were outside the dormitories. In fact, to make a visit to the toilet in the night was a bit of a hazardous enterprise, particularly for the women. The streets were patrolled by Japanese soldiers and there were a number of unpleasant occurrences.'

The camp was infested with parasites and vermin. Competitions were organised to stamp out the rats and anti-fly campaigns were held. 'There were mosquitoes buzzing about and giving us malaria,' recalled child internee Kari Torjesen Malcolm in her book, *We Signed Our Lives Away* (William Carey Library, 1990), 'and the bedbugs in all our mattresses that feasted on us at night. Hakon [her brother] counted 500 one morning in his bed. We poured boiling water on mattresses and furniture in a vain attempt to kill them. So we itched and scratched some more.' The usual method of killing the flat-bodied, red bedbugs was to run a knife or thumbnail along the seam of the blanket. Whatever method the inmates used to kill the vermin, they were fighting a losing battle – there were just too many of them!

Two of the worst aspects of camp life were the lack of privacy and space. Single men and women in the dormitories were allocated only 6 feet (183 centimetres) by 3 feet (91 centimetres) per person, and beds were only

18 inches (46 centimetres) apart. Married couples were given rooms measuring 13 feet (396 centimetres) by 9 feet (274 centimetres).

Not long after the establishment of the camp, the Japanese had put some of the families of four into two rooms, while others were forced to squeeze into one room. In an attempt to rectify the situation, Langdon Gilkey, as head of the Quarters and Accommodation Committee, suggested that the teenage children of four-person families be transferred to the dormitories under supervision. The rooms made available could then be given to those families in most need of the additional space. Confident that the former families would see the sense and humanity of this proposal, Gilkey approached first a prominent American missionary couple, Mr and Mrs White.

Initially, Mrs White was gracious and overflowing with concern for the plight of the families forced to live in single rooms. But when Gilkey suggested that her two teenage sons move into a dormitory for boys under the care of Eric Liddell, she became fiercely protective of her family's interests. Angry and disappointed, Gilkey realised his attempts to establish a more equitable distribution of rooms were futile.

Gilkey was disparaging about the businessmen in the camp, whom he considered flagrantly prejudiced and avaricious, but saved the full force of his acerbic wrath for the missionary community, citing incident after incident in which naked self-interest was clothed in pious morality. He described how Red Cross parcels arrived one day, each stuffed with sixteen packets of American cigarettes, presenting the missionaries with the moral dilemma of what to do with them. According to their sacrosanct principle of non-smoking, they should have destroyed the cigarettes, but as Gilkey observed, the majority of the missionaries gave in to the temptation to trade their allocation of cigarettes for tins of milk, butter, meat and other necessities with heavy smokers.

The dismal tirade continues until Gilkey comes to Eric Liddell. Often during the evenings, he would pass the games room and observe Liddell absorbed in a game of chess, making a model boat or organising some activity to try and keep the youth in the camp occupied.

George King, who entered the camp as a boy, recalled his first glimpse of Liddell. 'I was trudging wearily, laden with two heavy suitcases and feeling desperately hungry and tired after two bad days on a Chinese coastal steamer, down the rough path. We were being shown our dormitory, an empty, barn-like room, and were feeling utterly miserable. Suddenly, the person who was helping me along whispered, "Don't stare now, but the man coming towards us is Eric Liddell."

'I was too limp to connect the oncoming stranger with the "well-known" Olympic athlete of some years before, but I glanced aside to note the man on the path. He was not very tall, rather thin, very bronzed with sun and air. He was wearing the most comical shirt I had ever seen, though I was to get quite accustomed to similar garments in that place. It was made, I learned later, from a pair of Mrs Liddell's curtains. But what struck me most about him was his very ordinary appearance. He didn't look like a famous athlete, or rather he didn't look as if he thought of himself as one. That, I came to know in time, was one of the secrets of his amazing life. He was surely the most modest man whoever breathed.'

As soon as Liddell arrived at Weifang he was assigned to the school as a Maths and Science teacher, entrusted with organising the camp's sporting activities, and acting as warden for two large dormitories accommodating single men and women and children. He was also put in charge of the Christian Fellowship and became the camp's chief translator for the Japanese. On top of these 'official' duties, he voluntarily took on a myriad of tasks for the old, the sick, the infirm and the needy, including queuing for coal and rations and chopping wood. 'Eric wore his strength down doing this kind of work,' remembered an internee. 'I can see him now carrying 50 lb Red Cross parcels from the church to the homes of those who were old and feeble.' Remarked another: 'I recall seeing him plodding (that is the right word, for the camp diet took the spring out of even Eric's stride) up the camp road heavily loaded with buckets of coal dust and chips for making briquettes someone needed for a heater.'

According to George King, Liddell 'was without doubt the person most in demand and most respected and loved in the camp. One night he was telling how many hours he figured he did in a week and I was amazed that anyone could carry such a timetable.'

Joyce Stranks, a teenager in the camp, remembers Liddell being in such demand by the young people that his exasperated room-mates made a flip-card sign reading, 'Eric Liddell is in/out.' By turning the card to 'in' or 'out' Eric could keep the youth posted as to his whereabouts.

'One of my great moments in camp,' recalled child internee Kari Torjesen Malcolm, 'came when I was alone in a kitchen, singlehandedly trying to kill hundreds of flies before 600 people would file in for their rations. Then Eric Liddell was passing by. I knew him well, both as my softball coach and as a Bible teacher. Now he stopped in and gave me his undivided attention for a few charged moments. With his steel-blue, penetrating and laughing eyes and disarming smile, he had my complete attention. He told me that as a Christian I was bringing people nearer Christ by doing something as simple as killing flies for them. I had heard him teach that we either repel people from Christ or bring them closer. Then he heartily thanked me for what I was doing just then with no one but God to notice what I was doing, or to give me proper credit.'

Just as with his Anglo-Chinese College students, Liddell developed a close attachment to the young people in the camp. He devoted whatever spare time he had to organising activities to keep the children occupied, including chess and draughts tournaments, craft shows, plays and puppet shows. To encourage the teenage boys to keep fit, he would run round the camp perimeter with them and teach them running techniques.

'Evening after evening,' recalled an internee, 'he tore up, with a grim smile, all of the sheets his wife had left for his use, just to bind up the injured blades of the few precious hockey sticks which had somehow made their way into internment with us. He gummed the strips of linen with Chinese glue melted down over a one-candle-power peanut-oil lamp.

'It was fun to see him teaching them rounders! He arranged for the Americans to run a series of baseball matches, though he took no responsibility for any Sunday games.' With one exception. Camp policy was to have no games on Sunday, but a group of bored teenagers defied the ruling one Sunday and organised a boys versus girls hockey match. Without a referee, tempers became frayed and the match ended in a brawl. The following Sunday, Liddell was out on the field umpiring.

'Eric decided it was far more important that the youngsters played and worked together in harmony than it was to keep his Sabbatarian principles inviolate,' according to close friend Joe Cotterill. So the man who gave up the chance of winning a gold medal in the 100 metres at the Olympic Games, because he refused to run on a Sunday, was prepared to sacrifice his principles for the sake of fostering a spirit of peace and unity among the young people.

Liddell also spent considerable time giving extra tuition in Science to the older children who were hoping to go to university after the war. For one girl alone he spent hours painstakingly drawing Chemistry apparatus unavailable in the camp and she learned enough to win a place at Melbourne University as soon as the war ended.

An internee who was 18 when he was incarcerated wrote, 'Together with other young people I had the great privilege of listening to Eric, as a private tutor, lecture on Physics and Chemistry. As I recall his painstaking teaching methods, and his patience with me who was always slow to grasp mathematical formulae, I am amazed and grateful for this example of a superb teacher.' Another of Liddell's pupils remembers he transcribed a lesson onto a Christmas card which he designed and painted himself.

It was gestures like these, done quietly and without ceremony, that spoke much louder than words. Like the time he had a gold watch – presented to him in Edinburgh – weighed and valued in order to sell it to provide money to buy softball equipment, even though in the end it was not necessary.

Wherever there was pain and suffering, whenever a comforting word or a helping hand were needed, Eric was there. If the young, the frail, the infirm required extra food, he would offer his own meagre rations, without prejudice or discrimination.

Mrs Isabel Herron, who as a 14-year-old Isabel Harris entered the camp from Cheefoo school, recalled: 'When

Eric died, one of the women in the camp, a Russian pros-
titute, told my mother that Eric Liddell was the only
man who had ever done anything for her and not wanted to be repaid in kind. I think that when she first moved
into the camp, he'd gone and put some shelves up for
her. She was a woman living on her own; she didn't
have anyone to do that kind of thing. And it didn't matter what walk of life a person came from, Eric wouldn't
judge anybody . . . There were missionaries in the camp
who wouldn't have helped someone like her. But Eric
didn't see things that way.

'Missionaries,' continued Herron, 'can be people who
keep themselves so much apart. There were some people who were more interested in their own kind, and not
so interested in the others. And missionaries who didn't
really have time for these other people's children, and
just worked with the missionaries' children. But Eric
worked right across the board with everyone. It keeps
on coming across in my memory of him. He must have
been very strong, because he really did treat us all the
same.'

Norman Cliff, who was a teenager in the camp,
recalled another, less well-documented incident. A girl
called Marjorie Windsor contracted typhoid fever and
had to be isolated from the other internees. Only one
place was available to put her – the morgue, which
David Michell remembers as being just about the most
frightening place in the whole camp. 'The bravest
among us,' recalled Michell with amusement, 'would
poke sticks at the sheets covering the dead bodies, but if
someone left the door open and the wind blew the sheet,
we'd run like hell.' With her head brutally shaved,
Marjorie languished for weeks in the morgue, during
which time she witnessed the death of a Catholic nun
from the same disease in an adjoining bed. Without fuss

or fanfare, Liddell made a point of stopping by each day to read to her and try to bring a little joy into her traumatised life.

'No one could grumble long about conditions in the camp,' said another internee, 'as Eric would dismiss them with a merry twinkle in his eye, pointing out some amusing incident or something to be happy about. If, however, he feared some family relationships were going wrong, he would seek out people whom he thought could help and quickly secured their co-operation. His courtesy, good nature (which I never saw ruffled), with his unswerving devotion to God and principles, helped us to pass over many happenings which could have resulted in some nasty incidents.'

By the summer of 1944, internment was taking its toll on even the strongest. Besides debilitating physical diseases such as typhoid, dysentery and malaria, many inmates suffered from mental breakdowns and depression. As the tide of war turned against the Japanese, rations began to dwindle and the basic diet was increasingly limited to flour, *gao liang* (sorghum) and *lu dou* (green beans) and occasional poor quality vegetables and rotten meat. When even these ran out, and there was nothing but flour, the cooks invented bread porridge. They soaked stale bread overnight, squeezed out the water and mixed the foul mush with flour seasoned with cinnamon. Only the extreme hunger of the internees made it edible.

An average man requires around 4,800 calories a day in order to carry out heavy labour, yet the daily ration for men was reduced to 1,200 calories. The evidence of starvation was obvious – emaciation, exhaustion and apathy. Children had teeth growing in without enamel and adolescent girls were reaching womanhood without menstruating. In a desperate attempt to combat the children's calcium deficiency, some of the teachers, acting on advice from the camp doctors, washed, baked and ground eggshells into a gritty powder and spoon-fed it to the children. 'We gagged and choked and exhaled,' recalled Mary Taylor Previte with amusement, 'hoping the grit would blow away before we had to swallow. But it never did. So we gnashed our teeth on the powdered shells – pure calcium.'

Liddell was not immune to the effects of diminishing rations and a diet lacking in essential vitamins and minerals. Coupled with the tremendous workload and heavy responsibility that he took upon himself, malnutrition began to take its toll by the end of 1944 and contributed to the illness that was to take his life.

According to Marcy Ditmanson, Liddell started to get severe headaches and became forgetful. In an attempt to improve his memory and focus his concentration, he began memorising passages from Charles Dickens' *The Tale of Two Cities*. One such passage, remembers Ditmanson, was Sidney Carton's moving soliloquy before his execution by guillotine in place of a friend.

When Annie Buchan arrived at the camp some months after Liddell, she was shocked by the change in his appearance and how much he had slowed down. He was definitely 'losing ground' and had lost much of his bounce and energy. He also began to suffer from agonising headaches, forcing him to lie in his room, eyes bandaged and pleading for quiet. Recalls Joe Cotterill, who shared a dormitory with Liddell: 'Eric began to complain of headaches, which was unusual for him – about the smell of any little bits of food we cooked in the dormitory. We began to realise then that he was not well.' Despite the excruciating pain, Liddell continued to teach, counsel and encourage the youth, always there if they needed him.

In January 1945, Liddell suffered from a combined attack of influenza and sinusitis and did not respond to treatment as expected. When Annie Buchan heard of his deterioration, she marched straight to the men's dormitory in defiance of a camp rule which prohibited women. 'As soon as I had seen him I went straight to the head doctor at the camp and said Eric must be brought to hospital. He said there was no room. I said I thought Eric must have hospital treatment. So he was brought in. But he was so courageous, he would never say what he felt was wrong with him; so they just said, "Oh, he'll get over it."'

Instead, his condition deteriorated. While in hospital he suffered what was probably a stroke, resulting in the partial paralysis of his right leg, slurred speech and a wandering eye. The doctors suspected a brain tumour, but there was little they could do.

Appearing cheerful as ever, Liddell was reluctant to divulge his innermost thoughts. One of the few people he did confide in was Annie Buchan. The prolonged separation from Florence and the children, together with the terrible headaches, appear to have induced periods of depression. 'Many a time at the camp he was seen looking at the photographs of his wife and children,' recalled Buchan. 'One day he told me he couldn't see the future; everything seemed blank. He told me that he had one big regret, that he had not given Flo more time. And that wasn't like Eric; he had always been full of hope.'

Despite the continuing severe headaches, Liddell seemed to recover some of his strength and began to exercise his right leg. 'Eric had tea with my wife and family and we felt particularly sorry for him and others like him who had been separated from their families for so long,' reflected a missionary whom Liddell visited while still in hospital. 'As we were living in the top

storey of the hospital, with the boys of the China Inland
Mission school, we felt we might be able to brighten up
his convalescence. My wife cooked some little cakes, and
he asked the nurse to give him permission to climb the
four flights of stairs to our little room to see us. She told
him it was like "reaching for the stars", but with her support he successfully achieved his objective and sat down
too exhausted to talk.

'Eric's speech was very slow. It was obviously difficult
for him to talk, but he was quite cheerful and hopeful. His
will had quite clearly triumphed over his bodily weakness. He did not stay very long, but we invited him to
come and have tea with us two days later, on the Monday.
As we hurried away to a meeting, we marvelled that a
man so recently out of bed from a serious illness should
ever have been able to climb the stairs as he had done. We
looked forward to his coming again and we prepared for
him the best that our meagre camp store could produce.

'When he came he was looking better. The strange
look in one eye had almost gone. He was fully dressed.
He moved more easily. We sat and talked and he ate and
drank with us. We spoke of the way God had been dealing with him, and he told of the doctor's diagnosis, that
he had had a breakdown through bearing too heavy a
burden of work.

'Then Eric said something I shall never forget: "There
is just one thing that troubles me," he said slowly, "I
ought to have been able to cast it all on the Lord, and not
broken under it."

'My husband tried to reassure him, but how good it is
to know that such a one as Eric had not broken down
under the burden, as the diagnosis after his death made
fully clear.

'On the morning of the day on which he died, Eric
again climbed the stairs to return a plate on which I had

sent him something the previous day. A cheery word, a smile and the assurance that he was getting better. However, that evening Eric died.'

'At my camp,' wrote the wife of one of Liddell's Tianjin colleagues, 'I was cooking and supervising in the hospital kitchen, where we served meals for 150, all children under four and patients. Knowing Eric liked cake, I cooked him a "special" one day and sent it to him. He was thrilled. I saw him later, and he said he enjoyed it.

'Then he got out a little, and one day met me at 3.15, as I came off duty. He was taking a stroll, and I left the lady I was with to go over and speak to him. We walked for about fifteen minutes. He was his old cheerful self. "Have you heard from Flo?" I asked him. Oh yes, he'd had one of her letters and told me the news. He seemed tired and spoke haltingly. Not having seen him for several days, I thought he ought to be resting more. "No I must just get my walking legs again," he said. However, I took him in by the door for his tea, and that was the last I ever saw of him, for he died that evening.'

Three days before Liddell's death, Christine Helsby was in the camp hospital recovering from a near-fatal bout of typhoid fever. Liddell came into the women's ward to borrow a hymnal to check the accuracy of a hymn he was quoting in a letter to Florence. He spotted Helsby and flashed a cheerful smile in recognition. It was the last time she saw him.

Liddell dispatched his last Red Cross letter to Florence on 21 February 1945. The transcript read: 'Was carrying too much responsibility. Slight nervous breakdown. Am much better after month in hospital. Doctor suggests changing my work. Giving up teaching and athletics and taking up physical work like baking . . . A good change. Keep me in touch with the news. Enjoying comfort and parcels. Special love to you and the children – Eric.'

'The thing which disturbed me afterwards, although I didn't think about it at the time,' recalled Florence, 'was that his last letter was typewritten. He must have had somebody else do it. In the letter he said he had had a slight nervous breakdown, which I just couldn't believe of Eric.'

That morning he was gripped by a sudden paroxysm of choking and coughing. It seemed to pass, and he was laughing and joking again, when suddenly he was seized by another convulsion. One of his pupils, who was with him, ran out screaming for the doctor, who had Liddell transferred to a private room. Annie Buchan, who was just coming off duty, rushed to his bedside. 'I asked him how he was feeling, and he said no one had a clue what was wrong. That was the phrase he used – "They haven't a clue." After that I simply refused to leave. I stayed. One or two of the doctors were standing in the middle of the ward next door talking about Eric, and I just went in to them and said, "Do you realise Eric is dying?" Somebody said, "Nonsense." I went back into Eric's room, and by this time he was pretty far through. And he just said to me, "Annie, it's complete surrender." Then he took another convulsion and vomited all over me, and then he was gone into a coma and he never recovered.

'He was a man who'd been surrendering to God all his life and I don't believe it cost him much to say "complete surrender". You see, he knew where he was going.'

The next morning, an autopsy revealed a massive, inoperable tumour on the left side of his brain. Even if Liddell had received the most advanced treatment available, it would only have delayed the inevitable.

Eric Liddell died only six months before the camp was liberated in August 1945 by American paratroops. Mary Taylor Previte vividly remembers the day they arrived:

'Lying on my mattress in mid-morning, I heard the drone of an airplane far above the camp. Racing to the window, I watched it sweep lower, slowly lower, and then circle again. It was a giant plane, and it was emblazoned with an American flag. Americans were waving at us from the windows of the plane!

'Beyond the treetops, its silver belly opened, and I gaped in wonder as giant parachutes drifted slowly to the ground.

'Weihsien went mad. I raced for the entry gates and was swept off my feet by the pandemonium. Prisoners ran in circles and pounded the skies with their fists. They wept, cursed, hugged, danced. They cheered themselves hoarse. Wave after wave of prisoners swept me past the guards into the fields beyond the camp.

'A mile away we found them – seven young American paratroopers – standing with their weapons ready, surrounded by fields of ripening broom corn.

'Advancing toward them came a tribal wave of prisoners intoxicated with joy. Free in the open fields. Ragtag, barefoot, hollow with hunger, they hoisted the paratroopers' leader onto their shoulders and carried him back toward the camp in triumph.'

After three years of hunger, filth, squalor and vermin, of death and disease, the internees were at last free. Within weeks they would nearly all be repatriated to their respective countries. Children and parents, husbands and wives would be reunited. But they would never forget Eric Liddell.

12

SINE CERES

On a bleak, windswept morning in February 1945, Eric Liddell's coffin was lowered into a makeshift grave at the back of the camp. 'It can't be true; there's no way anyone like him could die,' cried the children in bewilderment. 'The entire camp, especially its youth, was stunned for days, so great was the vacuum that Eric left,' wrote a former internee.

'The wave of sorrow which swept over Weihsien was unbelievable,' recalled Meredith Helsby. 'His was by far the biggest funeral held in the two-and-a-half years of our stay in the prison camp.'

An internee who kept a diary jotted down on the day of Liddell's funeral: 'He was not particularly clever and not conspicuously able, but he was good. He wasn't a great leader or an inspired thinker, but he knew what he ought to do and did it.'

David Michell never forgot Liddell's explanation to the boys in the camp of the meaning of the word 'sincere', derived from the Latin *sine ceres* – without wax. If a Roman sculptor accidentally chipped a statue he was making, he would fill the crack with wax, which went unnoticed until hot weather melted it and the flaw was exposed. So a perfect work was one *sine ceres* – without wax. 'I always think of Eric as that true statue, a sincere man in every sense,' reminisced Michell. Indeed, Liddell once received a letter from one of his pupils signed, 'Yours without wax.'

The funeral service, held on 24 February 1945 and conducted by one of the camp's senior missionaries, the Reverend Arnold Bryson, united internees in a common desire to express their sorrow and grief for a man who had made their misery and deprivation a little more bearable. People who were not expected to attend were there – those previously not on speaking terms now stood side-by-side weeping unashamedly.

'I shall never forget that cold and windswept little mission cemetery,' wrote an Irish missionary who was at the graveside when Liddell was buried, 'where the whole camp family gathered and the young men carried his body to rest.'

'His funeral,' wrote one who was present, 'was one of the most moving events in the whole of camp life. Only a small proportion could enter the hall where the service was held, but in a quiet, unpremeditated manner it seemed as though everybody who could possibly manage it came and stood outside . . . During the short time he was with us here he had found his way into all our hearts.'

'Yesterday, a man said to me,' preached Bryson, '"Of all the men I have ever known, Eric Liddell was the one in whose character and life the Spirit of Jesus Christ was pre-eminently manifested." And all of us who were privileged to know him with any intimacy echo this judgement.

'What was the secret of his consecrated life and far-reaching influence? Absolute surrender to God's will as revealed in Jesus Christ. His was a God-controlled life and he followed his Master and Lord with a devotion that never flagged and with an intensity of purpose that made men see both the reality and power of true religion.'

Ten days later, the camp's Edwardian church was filled to overflowing for a memorial service led by old friend and colleague A.P. Cullen, who asked rhetorically why it was that no one had a bad word to say against Eric in a place which by its very nature created a daily climate of niggling criticism and back-biting. He reminded the congregation that it was the Apostle Paul who had instructed his friends to 'run to win'. In the spiritual race, said Cullen, Eric 'ran to win – and he won gloriously, didn't he?'

On the afternoon of his death, Liddell, maybe with a premonition of what was to come, had scrawled a few barely legible words on scraps of paper, including the first line of his favourite hymn, 'Be Still, My Soul', and that was what the congregation now sang softly as they stayed in their seats.

Years later, a letter was received by the British Broadcasting Corporation (BBC) from an internee requesting the same hymn to be played on a radio programme. 'I have no words to express the sterling quality of this wonderful man,' wrote the listener. 'He radiated patience, kindness and every possible virtue throughout our camp life. Although I am a Roman Catholic . . . I turned to him for comfort in my many hours of despair . . . Through his goodness and saintly example, he turned us from hopelessness and taught us what faith in God really meant.'

Another internee wrote, 'I was separated from my husband during the war years so I sensed what separation from wife and family meant to Eric Liddell, and I observed his peace and victory. My eldest son was

accidentally electrocuted some months before Eric's illness, and I recollect the comfort he brought to me in one
of our meetings, when he taught us that lovely hymn, "Be
Still, My Soul". . . Then again, as he spoke from the text,
"Be ye reconciled to God", he questioned if we were reconciled to God in all his dealings with us – not only in the
initial step of salvation, but day by day in our sorrows and
trials were we reconciled to God. So my memories of Eric
are of one who was quietly and victoriously reconciled to
God.'

'During the worst period of his imprisonment he was,
through his courage and cheerfulness, a tower of
strength and sanity to his fellow prisoners,' remarked
another. 'To many sufferers he brought the only comfort
that captivity allowed. It is one of the deep sadnesses of
life, that while so many survived the years of captivity,
E.H. Liddell, who had helped so many, did not. He was
one of the most chivalrous of Scots as an athlete and as a
man.'

'Unlike many missionaries,' reflected Marcy
Ditmanson, 'Eric seemed able to relate to everyone. Of
course his celebrity status made him welcome in any
conversation. But more than this, he had an unassuming, natural quality that gave him rapport with almost
everyone he met. Everybody regarded Eric as a friend.'

'Eric spoke with a charming Scottish brogue and more
than anyone else I had ever known, typified the joyful
Christian life. He had a marvellous sense of humour,
was full of laughter and practical jokes, but always in
good taste. His voice was nothing, but how he loved to
sing, particularly the grand old hymns of the faith. Two
of his favourites were "God Who Touches Earth with
Beauty" and "There's a Wideness in God's Mercy".'

'Eric so lived the Word,' said fellow missionary
Meredith Helsby, 'that when he spoke, it was with a

sincerity that made you feel he was speaking directly to you. His illustrations were usually from everyday life. He loved to draw observations he'd made in the chemistry lab. He often preached from the Sermon on the Mount and he emphasised the importance of putting Christianity into practice.'

His wife Christine remembers one such illustration. Liddell told those who listened, enthralled, of an evangelist in Australia who had spoken on Christ's triumphal entry into Jerusalem. After the service, a jockey came up to him and said: 'What wonderful hands Jesus must have had. If an untamed ass's colt came through a screaming palm-waving throng of people and yet arrived safely at the destination, the only explanation is the wonderful hands of Jesus.' Partly as a result of this realisation, the jockey committed his life to Christ.

And so the eulogies continued. 'The most Christ-like man I ever knew,' said a close friend. 'Thank God for Eric Liddell!' an internee at Weifang. 'The most famous, the most popular, the best-loved athlete Scotland has ever produced,' a fellow athlete.

Liddell's widow, Florence, was not informed of his death until more than two months after he died, when two friends of the family came to break the news to her at her parents' house where she was living with the children.

'I invited them in and I sensed there was something wrong,' recalled Florence. 'So finally I said to them, "Have you got bad news? Is it one of the boys?" (her two brothers). Even then, it never crossed my mind it would be Eric.

'About a month before the visit, I had had the strangest feeling. I was standing at the stove and I thought, "If you turn round, Eric is standing there." I could just feel vibrations. He was so full of life and bounce. And he said, "It's OK, Flossie. Everything is going to be all right." [Flossie was the name Liddell teased her with.] I thought my nerves were going. For three weeks I was conscious of his presence in this way. But it never crossed my mind that he had died. I am sure that somehow or other he was allowed to come back.

'I was terribly crushed when I got the news. I was all for jumping off the bridge. But again, his influence was just there, as if he were saying, "Florence, what are you going to accomplish by jumping off the bridge?" I was thinking I would catch up with Eric this way, but he would just look at me as if to say, "Flo, what about the three girls I've left in your care?" And that stopped me.

'Eric was ten years older than me. I'd like to have seen what he looked like today. He was eternally young, even though he had very little hair. He used to make jokes about it, but his mother was very perturbed and swore it was because he took too many showers.'

When Liddell died, Florence vowed never to marry again unless for love. Five years later, she did indeed fall in love again and had a happy marriage until the death of her second husband in the 1960s.

'But Eric? I consider myself privileged to have been married to him. We were married only eleven years, and for four of these we were separated. But I learned so much from him. It was a super marriage. He was a perfectly grand husband and so sweet with the children. Patricia, the eldest, has vivid memories of him, but unfortunately, Heather's memories aren't quite so vivid, because ever since she was ten months old, Eric was never with us for more than six weeks at one stretch.'

But what of the legacy of Eric Liddell? Stephen Metcalf, who still treasures a pair of battered running shoes presented to him in the camp by Liddell after he had noticed that Metcalf's were falling apart, is a man who can say, without exaggeration, that Liddell not only touched his life but changed it irrevocably. As a boy in Weifang, Metcalf had been deeply moved by observing Liddell's compassion for his captors, despite their brutality. Like so many of the incarcerated, Metcalf had developed a natural antipathy towards the Japanese. Liddell, in contrast, urged the internees to pray for and forgive the enemy.

After the camp was liberated in the summer of 1945, Metcalf returned to Melbourne, Australia, but could not forget Liddell's words. Then he heard a radio broadcast by General Douglas MacArthur appealing for missionaries to go to Japan to impart to a defeated nation the principles of Christianity, a task considered essential by MacArthur if the roots of democracy were to take hold. Metcalf responded to the call and, like his boyhood hero, Eric Liddell, gave up everything to become a missionary, spending the next thirty-eight years in Japan before retiring to Ireland.

THE MEMORY OF ERIC LIDDELL LIVES ON

The haunting wail of the bagpipes pierced the air as a lone piper, resplendent in tartan, played the poignant lament, 'On the Shores of Loch Katrine'.

The setting, however, was not the Highlands of Scotland, but a garden of remembrance at the back of a middle school in the northern Chinese city of Weifang, near the site of an old Second World War Japanese internment camp. Here, on the morning of Sunday 9 June 1991, forty people, including four former internees, gathered under a blisteringly hot sun to pay tribute to the memory of Eric Liddell who had died there forty-six years before.

Following a raucous cacophony of exploding Chinese fire crackers, heads were bowed in respect for a few moments as Dr Peggy Judge, Liddell's niece, unveiled a magnificent memorial stone – a one-tonne, seven-foot-high slab of Isle of Mull rose granite – inscribed in both English and Chinese, with a brief summary of his life and a verse from the book of Isaiah. Quiet, simple and understated – typical of the man himself.

Wigglesworth

The Complete Story

Julian Wilson

Few individuals have made such an impact on the world for the gospel as the Yorkshire-born plumber turned evangelist Smith Wigglesworth. Although he died in 1947, he is, arguably, more well-known now than when he was alive. He founded no movement, authored no books, had no official disciples, and no doctrine or theological college bears his name, but through his audacious faith and spectacular healing ministry, Wigglesworth fanned the flames of revival in many countries throughout the world. Thousands came to know Jesus Christ as their Saviour, received divine healing and were delivered from demonic oppression and possession as a result of his ministry.

In this biography, Julian Wilson provides one of the most comprehensive accounts of the life of Smith Wigglesworth to date.

978-1-86024-840-5

Authentic

We trust you enjoyed reading this book from
Authentic Media Limited. If you want to be informed
of any new titles from this author and other exciting
releases you can sign up to the Authentic Book
Club online:

www.authenticmedia.co.uk/bookclub

Contact us
By Post: Authentic Media Limited
52 Presley Way
Crownhill
Milton Keynes
MK8 0ES

E-mail: info@authenticmedia.co.uk

Follow us: